PASSIONATE
PARENTING

enjoying the journey of parenting teens

CARY**SCHMIDT**

First published in 2012 by Striving Together Publications, a ministry of Lancaster Baptist Church, Lancaster, CA 93535. Striving Together Publications is committed to providing tried, trusted, and proven books that will further equip local churches to carry out the Great Commission. Your comments and suggestions are valued.

Striving Together Publications
4020 E. Lancaster Blvd.
Lancaster, CA 93535
800.201.7748

Cover design by Andrew Jones
Layout by Craig Parker
Edited by Amanda Linder and Monica Bass
Special thanks to our proofreaders

The author and publication team have given every effort to give proper credit to quotes and thoughts that are not original with the author. It is not our intent to claim originality with any quote or thought that could not readily be tied to an original source.

ISBN 978-1-59894-209-5

Printed in the United States of America

DEDICATION

To my children—Lance, Larry, and Haylee:

Being your dad is a privilege and honor that I could never deserve! Your hearts for God have challenged me beyond words, and our journey together has been awesome but all too brief!

I love you more than life!

CONTENTS

ACKNOWLEDGEMENTS

I am so grateful to partner together with the greatest people on the planet! A book is very much a team effort, and I'm so grateful for the help that dear friends and co-laborers have invested into this project.

First, I thank the Lord Jesus for saving me and allowing me to be a parent! His grace truly is amazing!

Second, I am humbled to have married the most wonderful woman in the world! Dana, you're a fantastic wife and mother! Life with you is a dream come true. Thank you for being my companion in this wonderful adventure!

Third, I thank my kids. They have to put up with an imperfect dad who publishes stories—personal things—about himself and them, from which we can all laugh and learn. What a bummer for a teenager! Lance, Larry, and Haylee—thank you for supporting God's call on my life and for embracing Him and His will with true faith!

Fourth, I thank my own parents. Dad and Mom, you modeled so many of the truths in this book. I'm grateful to have grown up with what I wrote about! You're the best!

Fifth, I thank Pastor Paul Chappell—my pastor, my friend, and my mentor in so many areas. I've never seen anyone live out the principles of this book any better than him. Thank you for allowing me to have a part in Striving Together Publications!

Sixth, I want to thank the families to whom we've ministered. For twenty-two years, the families of Lancaster Baptist Church partnered with us in helping their children grow up in God's grace. We learned so much from their faithful examples! It was a joy to serve them, and God gave us many victories over the years. Also, thank you to the families of Emmanuel Baptist who have opened their hearts to us as we have begun ministry in their lives. We love you all and cherish the joy of watching God work in your homes!

Finally, I thank the Striving Together team. I miss working with you all on a daily basis! Thank you, Amanda Linder for your help in pre-reading the first and second drafts of this book. Your insight and expertise are invaluable. Thank you, Monica Bass for your editorial input, project oversight, and valuable encouragement along the way. Thank you, Craig Parker for a first-class layout. Thank you, Andrew Jones for a wonderful cover design. Thank you to the large team of proofreaders and others who make a project like this become a reality.

May the Lord use our collective efforts to encourage parents and families for His glory!

FOREWORD
from Dr. Paul Chappell

I first met Cary Schmidt when he was a teenager and I was his high school principal. Just before his senior year, our family moved to Southern California and I became the pastor of Lancaster Baptist Church. With his typical servant-hearted willingness, Cary jumped in the moving truck, helped us unload, and stayed for two weeks to help us as we got started.

To my delight, four years later, Cary and his wife, Dana, came on staff at Lancaster Baptist Church. For twenty-two years, the Lord gave us the privilege of working together as co-laborers in the ministry. And for the last twenty of those years, Cary served as our student ministries director and youth pastor.

The title *Passionate Parenting* is especially appropriate for this book because *passionate* is a good word to describe Cary and his passion for young people and their families.

He has a passion to see youth develop a personal walk with the Lord and love Him with all their heart, mind, soul, and strength.

He has a passion to help this generation of teenagers live wholly for the Lord in the midst of a perverse culture.

He has a passion to equip parents in raising their teens for God and for successful, godly adulthood.

He has a passion to see this generation of Christian families succeed in the core values of marriage and heart-level parenting.

And especially, he has a passion to help knit the hearts of parents to teens and teens to their parents—connecting both to God's design.

In short, Cary loves young people and loves their parents. In these pages, he will help you in the wonderful, but sometimes wild, journey of passionately parenting young hearts for God.

Paul Chappell
Lancaster, California
October 2012

INTRODUCTION
The Awesome Years

*Lo, children are an heritage of the LORD: and
the fruit of the womb is his reward.*
—PSALM 127:3

"Wait 'til they become teenagers!" Their tone was filled with dread. They were well-meaning parents of teens who were trying to warn my wife and me. We were young parents, and our first two children were still toddlers. They were in that "cute" phase, and life was difficult but fairly easily governed. As parents we were *clearly* in charge, and as children they were *clearly* dependent.

"They are cute and manageable when they are young—but *just wait!* Things *change* when they become teens!" Their long, drawn-out tones were mournful and burdensome—self-appointed, bearers of bad news called to warn us of the pending doom of our happy young family (cue funeral music…).

Eighteen years later, I am still waiting for the "dreadful" parenting days of which they spoke. Two decades into parenting and family—yes, things have changed—our kids have grown up all too quickly. Parenting has been tough at times. In seasons, it seems our kids have challenged us in more ways than we knew were possible. And yet, they are becoming wonderful adults with whom we love to spend time. The forewarned *dreadful days* never arrived. I'm sure glad we didn't believe those negative voices. Certainly that belief would have negatively impacted our attitudes and expectations of our family relationships.

Upon the arrival of the teen years, our family life and relationships grew more challenging but also more sweet and close. In our home—and in most healthy homes I know of—the teen years have been the most enjoyable parenting years (not to mention less work because our kids can now help with house and yard work). Through it all, they have truly become our best friends!

In great part, this book is a response to two things—a God-given, lifetime passion for parenting and family, and a request from young adults for me to reach out to their parents.

The Saddest Letter I've Ever Read

I received an unexpected letter from a young lady whom I had never met—a Bible college student who grew up in a Christian home and Christian school all of her life. I believe it's the saddest letter I've ever read and right on the mark for detailing the experiences of so many Christian families.

Please read it as it forms much of the foundation for the remaining pages of this book:

Dear Pastor Schmidt,

A few years ago, I read your books *Hook, Line, and Sinker, Discover Your Destiny,* and *Life Quest.* I found them to be extremely encouraging and instructive. These books showed me that not only do you have a real heart for young people, but you also understand us well. I am writing to ask you to consider writing a book to our parents and youth workers. Let me explain.

I am a junior at a well-known Christian college. I grew up in highly respected churches and went to excellent Christian schools. My father has been a Christian worker since before I was born. One would think that my testimony would go something like this:

"I was saved when I was about five and I had dedicated my life to God and I have been growing a lot and serving Him and now I'm studying to serve Him full-time." But that isn't my story. Actually, though I did make a profession of faith when I was very young, I didn't get saved until I was seventeen. Since I was twelve and now on into college I have struggled with "serious" issues. And I found out when I went to college that I am not the only "good kid" who is or has struggled with or is still struggling with serious stuff. We struggle with issues like eating disorders, depression and suicide, cutting, pornography, gender identity, homosexuality, drugs, drinking, immorality, and the list could go on. We listen to "wild" music, we idolize pop culture's heroes, we watch dirty sitcoms. We have no discrimination in our entertainment, dress, or any aspect of our lifestyle. Obviously, I'm generalizing our problems—you would not find that every Christian young person from a conservative background struggles with all of these issues, and praise God, some of us do not struggle with any of these issues.

My point is that the problems that are supposed to be bad kids' problems belong to us too. Unfortunately, our parents and youth workers don't know that we struggle with these things and they don't know what to do with us when they find out. Quite frankly, I believe that if you grabbed the average Christian school teacher or youth worker and asked them, "What would you do if you found out that one of the kids you work with was a homosexual?" they wouldn't know what to say.

My point is not simply that they don't know what we struggle with or how to deal with it. I think there is a pretty simple reason why "good" kids struggle with such serious stuff. And that there is a solution. At the risk of being blunt, I'm going to be blunt.

Our parents did not spend time teaching us to love God. Our parents put us in Sunday schools since K-4. Our parents took us to church every time the doors opened and sent us to every youth activity. They made sure we went to good Christian colleges. They had us sing in the choir, help in the nursery, be ushers, and go soulwinning. We did teen devotionals and prayed over every meal. We did everything right. And they made sure that we did.

But they forgot about our hearts. They forgot that the Bible never commanded the church [alone] to teach children about God and His ways. That responsibility was laid [first] at the feet of our fathers. Unfortunately, our fathers don't have time for us. They put us where we are surrounded by the Bible. But they didn't take time to show us that God was important enough to them to tell us personally about Him. So to us, Christianity has become a religion of externals. Do all the right stuff, and you're a good Christian. So, some of us walk away from church. Some of us stay in church and fill a pew. Many of us struggle with stuff that our parents have no idea about because they hardly know us.

I think these problems stem from first, our detachment from our parents, and second from our misunderstandings about the essence of Christianity—a relationship, not a list of rules. I worry that many young people like me are not even saved because of their misunderstandings about Christianity.

I know that this has not been a well-articulated treatise, but it comes from my heart. If you are able to help us and our families, we would be so grateful. I realize that probably, there is no way to fix the fact that kids my age are detached from our parents or to straighten out the crazy stuff that we struggle with. The alienation is fixed, the scars are permanent. I know our situation is not hopeless. God is at work in my life and my generation, among those of us who have struggled and are struggling. But maybe our younger siblings can have some help that we never had. Maybe you can write a book for our parents that will grab their attention and help them see that this is serious—that their kids need them, desperately.

All I could say when I read this letter was, "WOW! She nailed it!" This is the battle I've been fighting for more than two decades—in my own heart and family, as well as in ministry to other families.

Parents, are we teaching kids to simply *appear* and *act* right? Or are we teaching them to *love* God and *know* Him personally?

That letter and the accompanying plea has played out before me many times and in many ways—whether it's a ninth grade young lady shedding tears in my office over an absentee father, an eleventh grader describing his duffle-bagged, split-living arrangements between his divorced parents, or a college student seeking advice on how to respond to his parent's blatant sin.

Kids are longing for real, passionate, and biblical parents—not perfect parents, but parents growing in grace and sincerely following Christ. They long to see a genuine walk with God. They long for a connection with a transparent heart. They long to partner with growing and gracious authorities who will lovingly lead and passionately fight for them. They hunger for spiritually mature parents who not only love them—but who *like* them.

Considering the Letter

Before we move on, allow me to draw some critical observations about the letter and the problems it describes:

The problems described in the letter are universal among Christian families. This is not a set of problems that flow from a certain type of church or home. They are foundational problems that could be present in any home. Neglectful parents, fragmented families, and bitter children are the norm for our culture and society.

There is plenty of blame to share. Neither the letter nor this book is about finding blame. We could point at parental failures, marital failures, spiritual leadership failures, church failures, and ultimately to the individual—for we must all be accountable for ourselves. Let's just get it over with and blame Satan for his assault on godly institutions—marriage, the home, the church. And let's move on toward solution-based thinking. *Let's stop reacting to failure and start responding toward restoration.*

Everybody has a paradigm and a personal context. When I originally published the above letter on my personal blog, it provoked a lot of reactionary backlash. Many readers were of the opinion that every church (of certain types) is this way, or most families (of certain affiliations) are this way. And yet each wrote from their limited context. For it is absolutely impossible to throw a large blanket of "family failure" over Christendom or any one segment of Christianity.

Whether you come from a biblical family and healthy local church environment or from a broken one—there is grace, hope, and redemption to be found in Christ and the principles of His Word.

There are a lot of churches and homes doing it right. Through teen-parent meetings, family counseling, and fellowship in church, it has been my joy to know hundreds, perhaps thousands of parents and families over the years. In addition to this, I've been exposed to hundreds of churches and pastors. From my perspective, there are many people—pastors, parents, youth pastors—who understand this problem, grew up with this problem, and are fighting for a return to biblical foundations.

In my own local church, where I was the student ministries pastor over the past two decades, we were grateful by God's grace to see a large percentage (over 80%) of our young people remain faithful to Jesus after high school graduation and into their adult lives. And many of the 20% who wander spiritually eventually return to the Lord—we never give up loving, praying, waiting, and hoping for their recovery. We are always fighting and hoping for 100% of them!

Kids who grow up in the best of environments can still grow up and choose sin, reject God, and experience deep problems. I guess the ultimate proof of this is that people will choose to reject Christ at the end of the millennial reign (see Revelation 20:7–9). Imagine growing up during the millennial reign of Jesus Christ in a perfectly governed world. Even then, Satan will be able to deceive many and mount an army against Christ. The point is, it's not a matter of how I grew up, but where I will decide to go in the future and how I will respond to my past. Godly environments are no guarantee that an individual with a free will is going to make right decisions.

Finally, these problems are generational in nature. We're not dealing with new problems. For the most part, today's neglectful and disconnected parents are children of the same, and often their grandparents are too. Satan has been hard at work on God's idea of family for thousands of years. Healthy families have not been the norm for many generations. Many people today have simply never seen a healthy, biblical model of family life.

Some years ago I had an appointment with a father who had never talked to his teenage son about sexual matters—this is true of most fathers (and grandfathers). He was asking for help in how to do so. He said his father had never talked to him and he was unsure of how to approach this. (We will cover this in a later chapter.)

I was happy to help but was reminded again of the failure of past generations. I can't imagine a more important subject for a father and son to have a continual and close connection on, but very few actually do.

Where We Parents Lose Our Way

Please know I write these next words with fear and humility—for my wife and I have struggled on every one of these points many times. (Plus, I'm going to invite my kids to read these pages and critique me and Mom before it goes to press.) These words flow from one struggling parent to another. It would be impossible to avoid some of these imbalances 100% of the time, but if we are aware of them, we can work to stay sensitive, balanced, and engaged. Here are a few reasons we, as parents, lose our way:

We get too busy. In today's culture, this is *huge*! From work, to more work, to sports, to Internet, to a million other opportunities and obligations—we let events and information rule our lives. Like a large dog walking a small child, our daily agenda drags us around, and we fail to spend authentic, heart-to-heart time with our kids. The older they get, the easier it is, because they too become busy. Teenagers have sports practices, music lessons, youth activities, school trips, homework, projects, work, and on the list goes. We will examine this problem more closely in chapter 8.

We don't know enough, and we get intimidated. Let's face it, we parents struggle with knowing "how to parent." What do we teach? What do we talk about? How do we respond to our kids' questions, trials, and struggles? How do we make them comfortable opening up to us and sharing their struggles, and how do we help them when they do? Being "in over our heads" scares us stiff. Instead of asking God for wisdom and then courageously and compassionately dealing with situations, we ignore the problems because we don't quite know what to do. We will examine this more in chapter 11.

We find it hard to swallow our pride. Nobody knows our struggles as well as our kids. They see us at our worst. And sometimes, we as parents find it hard to make things right when we blow it. An authentic relationship, and a Christlike model, begins with humility. A humble parent is willing to own mistakes, ask forgiveness, and make relationships right. Many families carry a constant weight of unresolved conflict and past offenses—they were never dealt with or made right—so they just sit there like dead weight, dividing the hearts and burdening the relationships. We will look closer at this in chapter 4.

We do tend to focus on externals and behavior. In our busyness and rush through life, it is easy to get the idea that if everything *looks* good, it *is* good. Then our kids start to figure out how to "play the game." They think, *"If I look good, then everybody will stay off my back."* It's more of a natural drift than an intentional shift of focus. But this is where Satan takes his advantage in the heart. We will investigate this problem more in chapter 12.

We get tired or weary. Sometimes we're just tired, and we get lazy. After a long day, we want to come home and collapse. We feel it's our right to vegetate after an exhausting day's work, but it's then that our most important work should begin. Sometimes we're just not up to a late night discussion with our teenager—especially a stressful one. We have other plans! We throw up our hands in despair, walk away, and seemingly say, "Deal with it on your own, I'm too tired...." We will focus on this problem more in chapter 7.

We sometimes believe that providing the right atmosphere makes up for our failures. Good atmospheres like church and school and youth group are wonderful and biblical, but they are *secondary* to the home. They can really only complement or assist with what you are putting in place first. There is a strong tendency in today's Christian home to *deflect* spiritual responsibility onto outside people, organizations, and environments. Many parents feel that their responsibility is to provide food, shelter, education, and basic needs—and the "spiritual stuff" is the responsibility of the spiritual influences (pastors, church, school, youth group). This is a wrong way of thinking. We will look into this more in chapter 15.

We forget the power of our model. Parent, nothing speaks louder than our lives. Our kids need us to be real. If your children see you in love with Jesus, walking with Him, knowing Him, growing in His grace, and honoring Him—and then they *experience* that love flowing *toward* them *from* you—they too will most likely fall in love with Him. It's really that simple. Too many parents overuse their authoritarian, forceful control of behavior—to the neglect of Christlike love and genuine connectedness. We will see this more in chapter 2.

Do You Like Your Kids?

I know you *love* your kids—but do you *like* them? One thing is for certain—they have a very solid opinion on what your answer would be to that question, and that impacts every aspect of their hearts with you and with God. Imagine how demotivating it is if they feel that you love them but don't like them.

Sometimes I want to ask parents, "When did you stop *liking* your kids?" It's almost as if some families find every way imaginable not to spend time together as a family and not to enjoy their children.

Family life in a Christian home should be Christ-centered, close, loving, funny, enjoyable, memorable—something every young person craves! It's not natural for a teen to never want to be at home, or to be constantly holed up in their room, or to never desire to be around Mom and Dad. It may be culture's common model, but it's not what God had in mind when He created the family.

Parent, if you are looking for a magic formula to make parenting easy—some trick way to get your kid "in line" so you can get back to "your life"—this book isn't for you. You will be disappointed.

Bottom line, parenting is long, hard, heart work. It is an intense, loving labor of soul. It is a rigorous experience in sacrificial, selfless living. It is often exasperating. Most of the time my wife and I feel like we are failing more than succeeding—but the journey is wonderful with Christ at the center.

Are you ready to enjoy the journey of teen-parenting? Are you up for some hard work, some late nights, some "end-of-your-rope" moments, and some long and frustrating discussions? Are you also up for more laughter than you could contain, more great memories than you deserve, more love than you knew you were capable of, and more reward than you ever thought possible?

The pre-teen and teen years truly are the awesome years of parenting! If you're ready to discover a whole new level of engagement and enjoyment in your family, then let's dive in.

Let's give a whole new generation a million reasons to write a different letter!

A WORD TO SINGLE PARENTS

Parenting is a daunting challenge, but when God calls you to shoulder the task seemingly alone, the burden can appear almost impossible! May I share a verse with you, before you even begin reading the rest of this book? "Faithful is he that calleth you, who also will do it" (1 Thessalonians 5:24). You are not alone. Jesus Christ has called you, and He will enable you. You and Him are exactly what your child needs.

Whatever circumstances have unfolded in your family that have placed you in the position of being a single parent, I challenge you to trust God—cling to Him with all of your heart and soul. With single-minded faith and determination, fix your grip upon His truth and His presence in your family, and never let go. Never forget that you are not alone. Though you may consider yourself a "single parent"—you have an eternal Father who will carry you and your children through these wonderful and sometimes turbulent "growing up" years.

Throughout the coming pages, I write in reference to both parents, but the intent isn't to exclude the single parent. The truths of every chapter apply to each parent, and the biblical principles presented are applicable, no matter what your family structure. I hope you will find encouragement on every page!

Over the years, I have seen many single parents determine to follow biblical principles in their parenting. I wish I could share their stories of grace. In what seems like hundreds of cases, I've watched faithful single parents honor the Lord, cleave to Him, and bring up their children in the nurture and admonition of the Lord. I've watched those same children turn around a decade later and bless the sacrifice, the burden-bearing, and the passionate spirit of their single parent. Truly, God's grace can make up the difference and bridge the gap that is left by a parental absence.

Single parent, *Passionate Parenting* applies to you and your home. Your calling is great, but your God is greater; and—again—you are *not* alone! May the truths of these pages encourage you and help you enjoy the journey of parenting teenagers.

Part One
BIBLICAL
FOUNDATIONS

1

THE UNDERSTANDING PARENT
Proceed with Caution: Your Child Is a Mutant

"Who rode their bicycle through your mouth?" It was during my seventh grade year, and those were the first rather hurtful words I heard at Wednesday night Bible study when I arrived at church with my new headgear. As if braces and a retainer weren't enough torture, my orthodontist had to wire an erector set to my jaw! And even worse, he made me wear it *in public*! What a devastating thing it is to walk around with a hamster-sized Ferris wheel strapped to your face.

Then I remember the day I was asked if I was wearing water skis for tennis shoes. I was in seventh grade, and my feet had grown faster than the rest of my body, giving me that really cool "Ronald McDonald" foot look. If I had painted them red, people would have been asking me for autographs!

Then there was the "shrimp factor." In junior high, I was really rinky-dink sized! I think I was all of five feet two inches, while every girl in my class was nearing six feet. Why did I have to go to school with the "Amazons"? I was the smallest guy in the youth group—I couldn't even serve the volleyball over the net on a regular-sized court. My legs were so skinny that people called me "chicken legs," and I weighed ninety pounds dripping wet and bench pressed the same.

Identity crisis doesn't even begin to describe it. I was a walking mutant—a freak of nature—or so I felt.

Do you remember what it was like to be a teenager? For your teen's sake, you need to.

Most honest adults would rather lose a limb than have to go through that phase of life again. How easy it is to forget what life was like between twelve and twenty. How often we look into the eyes of a sixteen-year-old, and we see an adult, so we expect adult reasoning and responses. We tend to lose sight of the fact that there is a lot of transition going on in that teenage body and brain.

In the next few pages, let's relive those repressed memories. Let's think through exactly what your teenager is experiencing and how you can help. But first, realize the purpose of this chapter is not to cause you to have lower expectations regarding a teen's behavior or his capacity to live for the Lord. The purpose is simply that you stay mindful and prayerful of your teen's physical, emotional, and spiritual needs during some very tumultuous years.

God says in Proverbs 23:26, "*My son, give me thine heart, and let thine eyes observe my ways.*" I love how the father is asking for his son's heart. He was seeking a deep, connected relationship from which he could mentor, train, and nurture his son in the ways of the Lord.

How should we approach teenage transitions?

First, we should understand reality. If every cell of your brain was going to be completely rewired and replaced over the next eight years, wouldn't you like to know it? Wouldn't you hope others would extend some grace to you?

If you can identify with my story at the beginning of this chapter, the chances are, your teenager probably hasn't heard about it. Most teenagers do not feel that their parents understand them very well. While this usually is not the case, our silence is sometimes deafening. Why not spend some time reliving in your memory what those teen years were like—feel the emotions, replay the insecurities, and seek to truly understand your child.

Second, we should teach through these changes. While your teen probably has plenty of teachers, nothing can replace your guiding voice and gentle reasoning. A teenager cannot hear positive, affirming, comforting, and nurturing words too often. Make it your mission to help your teenager navigate these changes. Take time to talk them through the struggles, and ask the Lord to give you the insight you need.

Third, we should encourage and strengthen our kids through these changes. This may mean that you become a shoulder to cry on. It may mean you wrap your son into a big bear hug for a few moments. It may mean that you write your daughter a note telling her what she's doing right. You may need to call a big *time-out* on life so your teen can rest, recharge, and refocus. It will definitely involve prayer together on a regular basis, asking God to guide, guard, and grow His child.

Understanding Physical Change

Have you noticed how much your teenager is physically changing day-to-day and month-to-month? More importantly, have you considered the impact of those changes in all of life? As our boys crossed their thirteenth birthdays, I remember commenting to Dana how radically they would change in the coming years. These boys were about to quickly emerge as men. Never do teens change more quickly and radically than between ages fourteen and seventeen.

Sometimes we fail to acknowledge these changes (that often seem more like mutations) and to consider how they impact the world of our teens. They grow fast; that's a given. But consider the physical energy that is consumed to produce that growth. Consider the emotional impact of such physical drain. Connect the dots on the awkwardness, fatigue, hunger, and insecurity that accompany this radical physical growth.

No wonder your teen eats so much, sleeps so much, and seems to fumble around physically at times. No wonder they worry about what their friends think of them—they can barely keep up with the change themselves. Think about what radical physical growth produces:

Awkward coordination—Most young people go through at least a year or two of struggle in managing the rapid change of their growing feet and figures. What we see as immaturity or even clumsiness might simply be a fast-growing body where the mind and reflexes are playing catch up!

Clothing doesn't fit right—Clothing or shoes that fit well last week suddenly feel tight or cramped. That doesn't mean we give in to every "style-conscious insecurity"—but we should be sensitive to meet needs for clothing and shoes when the ones we bought three days ago truly don't fit anymore.

Physical features stand out—Teens generally walk around all day feeling "weird"—feeling like they stand out, stick out, or don't fit in. It's normal. Everybody's kids complain about these things—so don't over-react. The more you affirm them and encourage them, the sooner they will learn that this feeling doesn't represent reality. Most of their peers feel exactly the same way.

Personal hygiene becomes an issue—Have you taught your teenager the basic hygiene habits that adult bodies require? Well, it's time. If you don't, you are placing your teen at risk of some serious peer ridicule. Teenagers are ruthless on each other when it comes to smells and hygiene habits. Make sure your teen is ready.

Sensitivity to appearance—Have you ever had a bad hair day? A bad pimple day? Do you remember "not liking" the way you looked? Do you remember how frustrated you were at times with your appearance? (Maybe you should go grab your old high school yearbooks and let your kids laugh at you for a while.) Bear this in mind on those highly irritable mornings when the whole attitude and relationship seems like a train wreck.

Adult sexual desires become real—This is the time when childish minds occupy adult-ish bodies, and they don't understand the value of purity or know how to manage these new desires. It takes one-on-one parental, biblical training to nurture and protect them.

Rightly Responding to Physical Change

What does this information mean? It means we respond with wisdom:

Be patient in your spirit. All of this change should cause us to be more longsuffering and tender. Work your teen through it with patient training rather than rushed demands. Galatians 5:22 teaches that longsuffering and gentleness are fruit of the Holy Spirit.

Be understanding in your heart. When was the last time you sat down and encouraged your teen through these changes? Have you *ever* done this? If not, it's time. Let your teenagers know that you really do understand and desire to be there for them.

Be biblical in your training. Schedule time to sit down and biblically instruct your children through these times. Help them to understand the changes, and instruct them from God's Word. Be the initiator of these talks and have them frequently. Jesus is always a good starting point—*"And Jesus increased in wisdom and stature, and in favour with God and man"* (Luke 2:52).

Be balanced in your family schedule. Teenagers need about ten hours of sleep each night. That's not a preference; it's just a medical fact. Teen bodies require a good night's rest—if you want them to be in their right mind. Often a rebellious or antagonistic spirit can dramatically change with a good, long night's sleep. So often we miss the signals as parents—or we mistake them. Ask the Lord to help you understand the difference between rebellion and exhaustion. The first requires discipline, the second requires a soft pillow and an uninterrupted night's sleep.

Physical changes are real and they are massive! They impact the spirit, the heart, and the whole world of your teenager. Don't miss them. Don't forget about them. Be aware and be understanding. Ask God for daily wisdom to discern the difference between callousness and clumsiness, rebellion and fatigue, a bad attitude and a bad pimple.

Understanding Neurological Change

The most radical area of physical change is related to your teenager's brain. I know, you're already thinking, "Well that's obvious—mine don't have brains." And believe it or not, you're pretty close to the truth on that one.

Until recent years, there wasn't much medical evidence to explain what happens to a teenager's brain between the ages of twelve and twenty. But recent studies have provided some very conclusive and insightful findings.

Reason and judgment suspended—emotions take up slack: Have you ever heard of your "frontal lobe"? It's what helps you have reason and judgment—to be able to weigh consequences and to control impulses. Well, the truth is that your teen's frontal lobe is only now developing, which means teens tend to rely upon emotions and give in more quickly and easily to impulses. This is why teens tend to take greater risks with little thought of the consequences—like driving fast or engaging in extreme stunts.

For this reason, your teen needs your help in decision-making and your intervention to protect them from dangerous impulses. For all practical purposes, *you* are your teenager's "frontal lobe" until theirs is complete—which isn't until they are about twenty.

No wonder Satan attacks our kids and tries so hard to break down family relationships during these years—our kids are vastly more vulnerable because their brains are undercooked.

Brain under construction—thinking skills temporarily out of service: The Boston Globe reported on November 10, 2005, "Teenagers' brains aren't getting bigger as they grow: The brain cells, called neurons, are simply rearranging, making new connections, and pruning unnecessary ones to speed and reroute the flow of thought." Other studies have recently reported that every single brain cell is literally recreated and rewired between the ages of twelve and twenty. Think about it. What an astounding statistic! And all these years we've made such a big deal about losing baby teeth and growing adult ones—even to the point of getting money from the "Tooth Fairy." If a kid can collect a couple bucks for losing a tooth, how should we celebrate "growing a new brain"?

All of this tells us that the teen years are truly a time of "temporary insanity." Do you remember being so diligent to keep your toddler from self-destruction between the ages of twelve months and four years? If so, then welcome back to "survival-parenting" on a whole new level!

It is a medical, scientific fact that teenagers are undergoing radical, mental reconstruction, and this should call parents, pastors, teachers, and spiritual leaders to a new level of spiritual awareness and oversight.

The biblical connection that medicine doesn't make: Long before these medical studies were released, God's Word commanded us to engage in spiritual training during these years.

Deuteronomy 6:7–9 teaches, "*And thou shalt teach them diligently unto thy children, and shalt talk of them when thou sittest in thine house, and when thou walkest by the way, and when thou liest down, and when thou risest up. And thou shalt bind them for a sign upon thine hand, and they shall be as frontlets between thine eyes. And thou shalt write them upon the posts of thy house, and on thy gates.*"

Proverbs 22:6 teaches, "*Train up a child in the way he should go: and when he is old, he will not depart from it.*"

Here's where medical research falls short. What better time to ingrain Bible truth than during the very years when new brain cells are being developed and rewired? What better time to install "new software" than on a fresh hard drive? Truly, the teenage years are formational. These are the best years to increase spiritual development and to get God's Word into a newly forming brain.

As kids become teens, parents are tempted to disengage—believing that parental work is coming to an end. Wrong. Not only are teens vulnerable during these years—they are also *receptive* and *impressionable*. Rather than disengage, we should more fully re-engage.

Understanding Emotional Change

Have you seen your teenager recently experience a radical or sudden mood change? You know—one moment everything's fine, the next the world is falling apart. Have you seen an increase in frustration or sudden outbursts that look like anger or distress? Have you noticed that one day your teen can be on top of the world and the next day depressed and withdrawn?

Teenagers experience a wide variety of emotional changes, and often girls experience this more than boys. Their world has suddenly become more random and unpredictable than ever, and this can make them seem impulsive, compulsive, and even insane at times. (But then again, I know some adults who would fit nicely into those categories, so let's cut our teens some slack with understanding and guidance.)

Consider the factors that contribute to the emotional world of a teenager. More pressure at school, more responsibilities in life, a busier schedule, less sleep, and less family time all contribute to the emotions. (Not to mention teens who have endured abuse, broken homes, and painful trials.) Consider these emotional factors:

Changing relationships—Every relationship in a kid's world changes after the elementary years. Adults expect more from them at home and at school. Parents are often going through life changes as well, including marital, financial, health, and career pressures.

Desperation for acceptance and identity—Teens are more insecure and need acceptance more than ever. They grope for an identity in a culture that can't give it to them. Often they seek emotional stability in relationships and friendships outside the home, which can lead to destructive decisions.

Increased romantic attractions—Part physical and part emotional, this life-change is made worse by the assault of a culture obsessed with sex and perversion. Many teens become obsessed and emotionally dependent upon a boyfriend or girlfriend. Sometimes I call these relationships "mutual insecurity dependencies."

Fears of the future—Many young people are scared of adulthood. They long for stability, and their new "young adult world" seems much less stable than their elementary years. They see adults messing up their lives in painful ways. Many have witnessed firsthand the misery of failed marriages and broken homes. They fear growing up and doing the same, and they don't know how to chart a right course.

These are big factors! When one of these factors come crashing down on the heart, the result will usually be unpredictable and erratic emotions. Even writing this makes my emotions unpredictable!

So what do we do? How do we help our teens navigate this emotional blasting zone? Let me close this chapter by sharing a few ideas that we will see in greater detail in the coming pages.

Time with God and His Word—Ultimately all spiritual stability comes from building your house on the Rock! Identity must be found in Christ. The only way your teen will ever have true emotional stability is if he develops a personal relationship with his unchanging, loving Heavenly Father. As our kids learn to cast all their care upon Him, He truly will establish their hearts with grace (1 Peter 5:7, Hebrews 13:9).

Time with family—Parents, we need to postpone our mid-life crises indefinitely. There will be plenty of time for new cars, career promotions, and personal pursuits after the kids are grown. The God who gave you a family expects you to provide your teenager with adequate time together—the right kind of time. This is time that nurtures and settles the heart—time that talks together, prays together, and grows together.

Comic relief—God says that *"a merry heart doeth good like a medicine"* (Proverbs 17:22). Have you ever noticed how much teens like to laugh? It's what they do continually when with friends. I have seen teens laugh even in coping with tragedy. Laughter is God's gift to a young person learning to cope with the burdens of rapid life-change.

Identity, stability, and affirmation—Seek to help your teenager find his identity in family and God. Seek to give him stability at home and in life—by being faithful to your marriage and consistent as a mentor. Seek to fill her heart with kind words. Tell her what she is doing right and how important she truly is! God gave you to your child to help bring reason and stability to a world of unsettled emotions and questions.

Ultimately, we must teach our teenager to live life based upon truth (God's Word) over emotions (human feelings).

Are you an understanding parent?

Hopefully this chapter has reminded you what it was like—and with fresh remembrance, you can sit down with your teen and say, "Hey, right now, your life is hard—I get it. Here's how and why it's hard. Here's where you're headed. And here's how to deal with it. I know how you feel. It happened to me, too. Let's pray together!"

2

THE OBEDIENT PARENT
Hey Wait a Minute—What Kind of Kid Are You?

Before we can adequately talk about parenting—we need to take a look a little higher. There's a much more critical relationship at play in this picture called "the Christian home."

When you trusted Jesus as your Saviour, you became part of God's family. You chose Him, and He chose you—*forever.*

"But as many as received him, to them gave he power to become the sons of God, even to them that believe on his name...And because ye are sons, God hath sent forth the Spirit of his Son into your hearts, crying, Abba, Father" (John 1:12, Galatians 4:6). (Abba means "Daddy"!)

Birth is final. On that day, you became God's "kid," and He became your perfect, awesome, loving Heavenly Father—your spiritual Dad. I don't know what kind of family you grew up in or what kind of model you've seen, but if you know Jesus, I know what kind of Father you have now. He's perfect in every way, and He's ready to help you grow into His likeness as a parent.

The question of this chapter is simply what kind of kid are you? How is your relationship with your Heavenly Father?

Are you living under authority? Are you honoring your Father? Are you living in close fellowship with Him and seeking to obey Him in your life? Are you growing in His grace and wisdom? As God's children, we should be spiritually minded in all of these areas. Truly this is the very foundation of biblical parenting.

What You Do Is What You Get

There's a simple little principle at play in all of our parenting efforts, and our children intuitively know this:

How you live speaks louder and longer than what you say.

Your *model* outweighs your *mouth*. Your parental authority is established upon your submission to the Highest Authority. How you respond to your Father comes right back at you from your kids.

To the degree that you disobey and disregard your Heavenly Father, you legitimize your children's disobedience and disregard of you. If you live in disobedience, you discount your ability to expect obedience.

Now, I realize, children are commanded to obey their parents (Ephesians 6:1) regardless of the parent's spiritual state. Biblically, I have my kids "dead to rights" either way. And that position works when they are little—you know, the "because I said so" approach.

But this argument dies with the passing of the elementary years. For teens—*what you do* is king. What you say only matters if your life backs it up. Here's how they think:

Don't *tell* me—*show* me.

Don't *demand* it—*display* it.

Don't *push* me—*lead* me.

This shift in thinking during the early teen years catches a lot of parents off guard. And it's especially disruptive if you've developed the habit of living a duplicitous lifestyle—talking one way but living another.

Think about it. For the better part of ten or twelve years we are able to manage our kids' behavior simply by mandate. "Go to bed right now." "Eat your dinner." "Do your homework." Because our role as parents is so big in their eyes and they are so dependent, they really do *have* to do what we say—no questions asked. Our influence can be more about dominance than example. And so we tend to settle into a control mode which manages behavior but doesn't model it. We can default into merely issuing demands rather than mentoring the heart. We can lead by dictating rather than doing—it's easy when they are young.

Suddenly, the teen years hit like a tidal wave and shatter our well-controlled parental universe. As teens, our kids start using their newly wired brain cells to rethink everything. They start subconsciously connecting dots and reprocessing years of parental authority. It hits them one day that *we are kids too*—and that we have a much higher Parent to whom we give account. For a strong-willed child, this challenging spirit may come even earlier in life.

Then, the pesky little critters start examining us—actually thinking about how we live and drawing their own conclusions. (How dare they!) What they find leads to a whole new world. They study what we watch, listen to, and say. They examine how we treat God, our spouse, our church, and our job. They investigate and find interest in every little detail and behavior of our lives. They place us under the microscope of consistency—essentially asking this question:

"Is this God thing real to Mom and Dad? Should I really take this seriously?"

Sadly, when teens come up with a negative answer to that question—when they see a life that doesn't back up the talk—they quickly disconnect from developing their own faith.

God's Word is fertile ground for seeing this played out. Isaac knew God was real to Abraham, and Jacob knew God was real to Isaac. Solomon and Absalom knew God was real to David, but they also watched him dishonor God in family life—repeatedly and for long periods of time. And in the end they both self-destructed.

And Solomon's son Rehoboam? He watched Dad play. He watched Dad turn from the Lord God to sex (as a god) and idolatry. He watched Dad give his life to foolishness and vanity (Ecclesiastes 1:17). He watched Dad reduce the Almighty God of the ages to just another god on the shelf of many. And so, he walked away. Why bother? Solomon invited his son (at some point in his life) to watch his life—"*My son…let thine eyes observe my ways*" (Proverbs 23:26). Too bad he later left his own advice.

Parent—what kind of *kid* are you? Are you chipping away at your moral authority and influence in your child's life by disregarding your Heavenly Authority? Do your children see you obeying or disobeying God? Do they know you honor God no matter what, or do they see you playing around with sin and foolishness? Are they seeing you go through the motions of worship on Sunday and then dabble in things that dishonor all week?

If they are watching you disobey your Father, you are creating a moral dilemma in their hearts that will manifest itself in various unpleasant ways in your home and in their futures. This is an unstable, fractured way to parent, and it reaps a really bad harvest.

Remember, our kids don't expect us to be perfect—just real. If your children see you loving and obeying your Heavenly Father, they are much more likely to do the same. And they will find it more logical to obey you in the process. After all, obedience is what they see in you.

It's really that simple. If you passively or inconsistently love God, then they will probably disregard you *and* your God. Your parental expectations will be rebuffed by hardened hearts. You will experience an absolute loss of parental credibility.

In family counseling, I often find it odd that *disobedient* parents expect *obedient* teens. It's just not going to happen—not for very long anyway.

Into the teen years, too many parents try to overuse their authoritarian control of behavior. They forget that they are dealing with fresh brain cells that are now asking "Why?" They forget they are dealing with young adults who suddenly find new courage to cry "foul" when they see one. And if you are living in obvious (or hidden) disobedience to your Father, they most certainly *will* cry "foul."

So What Are We to Do?

To put it simply—if you want obedient kids, *be one.*

If you want deceptive kids, be one. Disobedient kids, be one. Argumentative kids, be one. Defensive kids, be one. You get the point....

You are modeling *childhood* to your child. You are also modeling parenthood to your child. They will learn how to be a kid from you, and they will learn how to be a parent from you. So swallow hard, dig deep, and…uh…yep, I'm going to say it: *straighten up! (And go clean your room while you're at it.)*

Have the relationship with God that you want your kids to have with you.

Love Him, and they will love you—and Him. Obey Him, and you have every right to expect obedience and to deal with disobedience. Honor Him, and you should receive honor. Have a right heart with Him, and you can lead your kids to have a right heart with you. Deal honestly and biblically with your own failure, and you can help your children deal honestly and biblically with theirs.

Parent, you and I are just a link in the chain of authority. We are *under* authority, and modeling obedience is the best way to teach it and receive it. Standing on the solid ground of submission is the best place from which to teach submission.

Here's your assignment in becoming an obedient parent:

Pursue God and love Jesus with all of your heart. Ephesians 6:6 reminds us to do the will of God from the heart. God tells us His first command is that we *love Him* with all of our hearts.

Your children know what (or whom) you love. It's only obvious in your lifestyle. And don't think you can fool them. If you love God intensely, they will know it. If you love Him casually, they will know it. Your life is your loudest message. Your life is your truest message.

They will mimic what you model. And they will view your whole life and your authority through the lens of your authenticity. If you are authentic, your parenting authority will have credibility—and with teenagers, if you don't have credibility, you have nothing. Credibility is king in this relationship.

Obey your Heavenly Father and let your kids know. Are you faithful to church? Are you growing in God's Word? Are you listening to God and making changes in your life based upon His internal conviction? Then show it to your kids. Talk about it. Sit down at the dinner table tonight

and say, "Hey, you know, God's been really speaking to my heart about…
and He's challenging me to obey." For instance, do you tithe? If not—
start. And when you do—tell your kids.

Your kids should see obedience to God throughout all of your life.
It should be obvious. And the biblical answer to most of their questions
could be, "You know, I don't do that (or I do that) primarily because I'm
trying to obey God." That also works when your decision is that they
can't spend the night at a friend's house or go to the birthday party they
wanted to attend—"Sweetheart, I know you don't understand this, but as
I'm praying about it, God is saying 'no' and I'm not really sure why, but I
have to obey Him."

How can teens argue with that? You are obeying your Father. If they
have a problem, it is with God, and they can appeal to Him.

So much of life really just boils down to listening to God and obeying
Him. And when He's silent, we need to keep obeying His last command.
In our human psyche, we need to explain it all. We need to logic it through
and have strong rationale for every decision. Sure, sometimes thinking
things through is wise. But a relationship with God isn't usually logical,
and obeying Him isn't always explainable by human rationale. Obeying
Him is hearing what He says and doing it by faith.

Don't get caught in the appearance trap. Don't play a game
spiritually. Too many parents act one way at home—rather unspiritually—
and another way at church—spiritually. Too many kids see their dads
pray with men at church, but never with the family at home. This game
doesn't work in leading teens. They see straight through it, and they
resent it. They use it to justify bad attitudes and negative behaviors. One
of the worst things we can do as parents is indirectly give our kids more
ways to justify their own sin.

Parent, externals are just that—*externals*. They are to be the product of a right heart, not a replacement or cover for it. Whatever outward service or standards you have in life, let them flow from a fervent, heart-based love for Jesus Christ and solid biblical obedience to your Father. When your kids ask "why," be able to answer, "Because I want to obey God." That's a rock solid answer for a child of God.

Let your life flow from the inside out. The externals of the Christian life—the preaching, teaching, worship, service, lifestyle—only make sense to your kids if you have a genuine heart walk. You can't hide or mask a genuine love and walk with God. It just comes out of you on every level of human relationships, and God uses your delight in Him to make Himself more attractive to your child.

Prove your beliefs and biblical standards. While externals do not produce spirituality, a truly spiritual heart will always show externally. You can't hide godliness beneath a carnal exterior. Our kids need to see us growing in obedience and commitment to Christ. It starts in the heart, but it flows into all of life.

A growing child of God will be seeking godliness and holiness in life, and our kids are looking for behavior that is driven by biblical belief. If it's real with you, then they will know it. You will be able to answer for it. And you'll have a good case for helping to make it real with them, too.

Titus 2:11–12 states that the grace of God teaches us to deny ungodliness. God's Word is clear that our conversation (lifestyle) is to be as *"it becometh the Gospel"* (Philippians 1:27). And we are commanded to *"shew forth the praises of him"* (1 Peter 2:9).

Decide to be an open, approachable parent. Does the thought of your kids examining your life bother you? If so, why? Probably because there's something you don't want them to see. We will examine how to deal with our sin and parental failures in chapter 4, so hold that thought.

For now, just consider the fact that God has placed these young humans in close proximity to you on purpose—for quite a while. He knows your failures and flaws, but apparently that wasn't enough to disqualify you. Perhaps He intends for you to model honesty, transparency, confession, and repentance as well?

Don't be tense about letting them inspect your life. To the best of your ability—given that you still struggle with the flesh too—seek to be real and be right. Our kids, of all people, know we are flawed. Nobody ever grew up with perfect parents, and they know that. But we *can* be genuinely in love with God, in pursuit of Christlikeness, and under the control of His Holy Spirit.

Welcome their examination. Welcome their questions. And be prepared to be greatly challenged at the deepest level of your belief and practice. Be prepared for your every inconsistency to be exposed that you may deal honestly before them. For all their missing brain cells, teens sure can come up with the most profound and insightful questions. They sure are great referees and quick to throw flags!

For all their emotional fog, they sure can see through us clearly.

The Christian life *makes sense.* A holy life *makes sense.* Right living is worth it. Make sure your kids can come to you with "why…?" and "how come…?" and "but what about…?" And when they do, give them solid, biblical, logical answers. And back up your answers with a life of obedience.

When it comes to teen parenting, start with this question: What kind of kid am I?

Build your authority upon the solid foundation of submission to your own Heavenly Father. Teach your children to obey you because you obey. Show them what it looks like. Teach them how to do it. Model submission before you demand submission. Then expect obedience and hold them to the commands of God's Word.

It is morally inconsistent to expect obedience that you are not willing to give.

3

THE AUTHENTIC PARENT
Calling All Game Masters

We took a group of twelfth grade teens out for a game of laser tag recently. The adventure unfolded in a dark maze thickened by fog and black lights—it was all essentially designed to completely disorient the players. Sounds fun, huh? Actually, it sounds somewhat like life!

Prior to the game, our group was called into an orientation room. There, a kind-hearted young lady explained to our over-enthused, well-caffeinated group that she was "the game master." This meant she was the final authority over the maze. She was there for our protection, for our accountability, for our information, and for our care.

Early in the orientation she issued some clear boundaries—no running, no physical contact, no rough play, etc. "You run...you're done!" she threatened. But she also issued some blessings—"If for any reason you get lost, feel completely disoriented, alone, or need help, please raise your laser gun high into the air with both hands and cry out, 'GAME

MASTER!' And I will be there to help." (We won't go into whether or not I felt disoriented during the game.)

"Game master." What a great term. *Keep me safe, help me know the boundaries, and lead me through the fog.* In a way, that's what we all need in life. That's what your teen needs from you—biblical authority that provides safety, leadership, and care.

And yet we face a great dearth of "game masters" in today's Christian home. Authority in post-modern culture is in many ways broken. Let's briefly examine it:

Authority—Authentic

Have you ever considered the relationship between the words *authority* and *authentic*?

The word *authority* comes from early Latin roots signifying something that came from a factual, original source in settling an argument.

The word *authentic* comes from early Greek roots meaning "original, genuine, not fictitious."

In present day secular culture, the word authority often has negative connotations. Sometimes we hear the mantra "question authority"—a phrase implying rebellion. In actuality, when considering the root meaning of the word, questioning *authority* should be a positive thing— as in, go to an *authentic* source of *truth* and get your *authoritative* answers.

Today the word *authority* implies the use of power and sometimes its misuse or abuse. How desperately we need a biblical understanding of parental authority—the kind that cuts clearly through the lies of the enemy and provides a settled foundation of truth and stability.

If you're going to enjoy parenting teens, you must understand God's original intent for your role and expression of parental authority.

What Is Authority?

To put it simply—*Jesus is authority.*

Jesus is the ultimate and eternal authority of Heaven and Earth for the ages to come. All power is His (Matthew 28:18). All truth is in Him. He is the settling of every argument, the standard of every measurement, and the truth at the end of every question. Jesus is authority. All earthly authority flows from Him, is ordained by Him, and is under Him. He is the head of all things.

"*For by him were all things created, that are in heaven, and that are in earth, visible and invisible, whether they be thrones, or dominions, or principalities, or powers: all things were created by him, and for him: And he is before all things, and by him all things consist. And he is the head of the body, the church: who is the beginning, the firstborn from the dead; that in all things he might have the preeminence*" (Colossians 1:16–18).

The source of all power and all truth—all authority—is Jesus Christ. Therefore *biblical, parental authority is simply the life and power of Jesus flowing through you for the benefit of those under your care.* Expressing authority—in its purest sense—should be one of the most Christlike things any parent can do.

In the light of this thought, what does biblical authority—*the life and power of Christ flowing through me for the benefit of those under my care*—look like?

Three Typical Expressions of Parental Authority

For the sake of clarity, I want to describe three styles of parenting. Which one of these is most like you?

The passive parent—We will examine this in greater detail in chapter 7. The passive parent basically relinquishes authority to the child. This is truly a "child left to himself"—*"The rod and reproof give wisdom: but a child left to himself bringeth his mother to shame"* (Proverbs 29:15). This sort of parent fosters resentment and rebellion in the child because their typical posture is "I'm too busy, too tired, too distracted by other things to love you and engage in your life. You are an intrusion into my life."

The oppressive parent—This parent is on a power trip of authoritarian control. This is carnal authority expressed with overbearing demands, loud dictates, and stern force—even if it is well meaning. This parent is stuck in the "because I said so" mold—expecting blind, automaton obedience. This authority rules and manages behavior, but it breeds resentment and rebellion in the heart. It says to the child, "I don't care about you, I care about me! I care about having control. I care that you do as I say." *"And, ye fathers, provoke not your children to wrath…"* (Ephesians 6:4).

The authentic parent—This parent seeks to be genuinely like Jesus in the expression of biblical authority—strong in truth but also tender in love—balanced. This authority is genuinely tied to what is true and real—not merely putting on an outward show of strength or authority, but authentically expressing the love of Christ through biblical direction. It is meek (power under control) but also firm. It is the biblical use of power for the benefit of those whom God has entrusted to me. It is leadership that leads the right direction, sets the right boundaries, and expresses the right care. "*…but bring them up in the nurture and admonition of the Lord*" (Ephesians 6:4).

Which one are you? Which one would your teenager say you are?

Passive?—meaning they are mostly left to themselves, their rooms, their devices, their friends?

Oppressive?—meaning they have almost no opportunity to think for themselves, and they think your *loud* voice is your only voice?

Or Authentic?—meaning you remind them of how Jesus would live. You are Christlike in setting the boundaries, setting the example, and setting the course.

The goal is *authentic*—Jesus is authentic. He is truth. *Biblical authority is authentically like Jesus—taking dominion with humility and using it in love and grace for the benefit of others.*

Qualities of Biblical Authority

Let's quickly examine nine qualities of biblical authority:

Biblical authority provides order—we serve a God of order who created a universe of order and commands us to do all things decently and in order (1 Corinthians 14:40). Order provides a structure in your home and family life where authority and growth can play out. Without order, everything comes unraveled.

Disorder leads to chaos—emotionally, relationally, and spiritually. Many homes function in continual chaos because they are in a state of perpetual disorder. *Order leads to calm*—emotionally, relationally, and spiritually.

Take a look at your home, your living spaces, your schedule, your car, your child's bedroom, and ask: In what ways is this home in disorder? Can I create a more ordered environment?

Biblical authority is meek—In Philippians 2:8 we read that Jesus "humbled Himself." The final Authority of the universe humbled Himself and became obedient. He gave Himself as a sacrifice to redeem us to Himself. This heart attitude must preside in every authentic parent—"I am entrusted with authority by my Saviour to bring His power and love into expression in the lives of my children. I am nothing, and Jesus is everything."

Biblical authority provides a protective environment—Just as our national justice system (even with its flaws) is designed to protect and provide safety, so biblical authority exists to provide the same. As our *"heavenly Father knoweth that ye hath need of all these things"* (Matthew 6:32), even so, a godly parent is a providing, care-giving, protective parent.

Biblical authority models right behavior—As an authority, my example is more powerful than my demands. My first obligation is to live in the way that I expect my child to live. For instance, if I have a short fuse and a tendency to lose control, I'm modeling bad behavior—essentially justifying my child's tendency to do the same.

Authentic leadership simply says, "Watch me. Before I expect you to behave in a certain way, you will see it in me. And along the way, let me explain why we do it this way. It all comes back to Jesus…."

"Those things, which ye have both learned, and received, and heard, and seen in me, do: and the God of peace shall be with you" (Philippians 4:9).

Biblical authority nurtures the right behavior—It thinks this way: "As a parent, I will not *expect* of you what I have not *taught* you. If I have taught it, then I will expect it." You cannot hold someone accountable for behavior you have not taught.

How often do you expect behavior or thinking from your children that you have not personally instructed in their lives? This has happened to me more times than I can count.

Too often our carnal parenting process looks like this:

1. Demand it.

2. When failure occurs, get angry and repeat step one louder.

In truth, a spiritual parenting process should look like this:

1. Do it.

2. Teach it.

3. Expect it.

4. Reward it.

5. When failure occurs, biblically deal with it; then go back to step one and repeat process.

How often I have found myself on the carnal path! And usually the Holy Spirit convicts by saying, "Shouldn't you *teach* this first?" Should our kids just automatically "know better"? Not unless they have seen better and been taught better by us.

Biblical authority is motivated by "what's best for you"—"I am seeking your best interest." Living under right authority is going to help your child, not just you. Our kids can see through our motives.

For instance, when a parent yells, "Shut up in there, I'm trying to watch the game…"—that parent is expressing power and control, but not authority. This is merely an abuse of authority, driven by self-centered control. Our kids intuitively know the difference between the exertion of power and the expression of biblical authority.

Every parent wants happy children—but God's first goal is not to make us *happy*. It is to make us *holy*. He is transforming us into the image of Christ, and sometimes that's unpleasant. Even so, Christlike parents are motivated first by what is *best*, not what is most pleasant or most convenient.

Biblical authority employs right discipline—Too often parents discipline out of anger and for selfish motives. Right discipline is *corrective* and *restorative*. It is not merely *punitive*. Right discipline is controlled, premeditated, and designed for growth. (More on this in chapter 19.)

Biblical authority expects responsibility—If I am modeling and teaching responsibility, then I can expect to see my children grow in responsibility. With every passing year, they should take greater responsibility for themselves—their homework, their walk with God, their chores, and their commitment to courageously make right choices.

Biblical authority earns respect—You could demand respect as a parent, but you really shouldn't have to. Respect is a natural by-product of living respectably. And, while there is no excuse for disrespect toward parents, often that disrespect is rooted in offense. Often a teen feels justified in their disrespect because of some behavior in their parents that they feel is not respectable.

You could ignore the root issue and demand respect. Or you could sit down face-to-face with your teen and explore the possibility that there is an offense or an inconsistency in your parenting that is acting as a wedge in your relationship.

Biblical authority never makes an excuse for rebellion, but it always earns respect by living respectably.

Taking Authority Is Taking Leadership

This really boils down to leadership—parents stepping up and leading the home in the direction of Christ. Notice I didn't say "pushing," I said "leading." It's easier to push the kids into surface behaviors than it is to lead them toward heart transformation.

Take another look at those qualities of Christlike authority. This type of authority is hard work and requires the sacrifice of time and effort. It talks through tough times, even late into the night. It changes its personal plans on a whim when a critical need arises. It takes advantage of teaching moments even when it is tired. It stays engaged even when it is reviled or scorned. It is selfless, always laboring for the well being of another. And it fights tough battles for the safety and protection of another—especially when those others are opposing themselves. Here's how God's Word describes it: *"In meekness instructing those that oppose themselves; if God peradventure will give them repentance to the acknowledging of the truth"* (2 Timothy 2:25).

What about Rules?

I often speak to parents who are afraid that too many rules will cause their child to rebel. This sounds like the right track. The reasoning makes sense—"Box me in too tightly, and I will eventually try to break out." And yet, it's not the rules themselves that are the problem.

The relationship—or lack of one—is the real problem. I have never seen a teen rebel and walk away from God simply because of "rules." It's often more about a parent, in the context of a broken or neglectful relationship, trying to unreasonably enforce rules.

Think of it this way—in a healthy relationship, where parent and teen are close, the rules take on an entirely different dynamic. In this case, the rules are not focused on control or behavior modification. The rules are not captors holding the teen hostage. In a healthy relationship, the rules are protective boundaries or guardrails. They are biblical, well-reasoned, and they serve a clear purpose in honoring God and guiding and protecting life. In healthy relationships, the rules are secondary to the heart connection. The rules are a structure that simply supports the healthy relationship.

Kids who rebel—even those who say it's about the "rules"—are really crying out that they never understood the rules, never had clarity on the benefits of the rules, and never had the relationship for which they longed before the rules. Their unsettled hearts lash out to blame the first apparent culprit, and often the rules get a bad rap. Quite often, the outward rebellion is simply a cover for a wounded heart, and the hurting person is merely attempting to return hurt in the form of rebellion.

It's often been said, *"Rules without relationships breed rebellion."*

Teens are more than capable of having beneficial boundaries carefully explained and lovingly enforced. Their hearts deeply crave this because they intuitively know that true love must also be tough love—protecting love. Their brains reason it this way, "If you are my authority, and you have no rules or boundaries for my life, then you just don't care about me." Even when they protest the rules, somewhere deep inside they appreciate a parent's consistency in enforcing the rules and caring for their well being.

Any strong relationship will have boundaries. It's that simple.

For instance, if my marriage is to be strong, it must have boundaries. A good marital boundary is that I don't spend time alone with other women. That boundary doesn't *make* my marriage strong, but it surely protects it so that it *can be* strong. Boundaries are not standards of legalism, they are merely rules of conduct that protect the relationship—that create a structure or framework within which a strong relationship can exist. If I love the relationship—the person—there are certain things I will do and will not do—if only to please the other person. Such is our relationship with God. The behavior, the "faith in action," along with the boundaries, should flow from a heart that is deeply in love with and close to Him.

Loving Him is the only real and lasting motivation for living a godly lifestyle. The Bible is very clear about God's desire for us to live lives that are holy, distinct, and separated from the world. Those "standards" or "boundaries" are designed not to create mere performance or outward conformity, but to flow from and facilitate a continued strong personal relationship with the Lord.

Even so, in a Christlike home, biblical authority is a beautiful blend of truth and grace. It is a balance of loving relationships and beneficial boundaries.

The love and truth of Jesus should be the overriding, presiding presence in your family life, and it should flow from your genuine walk with Christ as a parent. The hearts of our kids blossom with life in the light of such a relationship. This sort of biblical authority in the Christian home is truly a taste of Heaven—certainly not perfect or conflict free, but at least healthy and whole.

Passionate parents understand, humbly accept, and graciously express *authentic* authority. They embrace the role of "game master." They aren't afraid to be firm (i.e., "You run—you're done") But in a time of confusion, they are also there to run to their child's side and help them find their way. Boundaries? Yes. Blessings? Yes. Benefits? Yes. Biblical authority provides all of these.

Now it's your turn—take this chapter and teach it to your teenager. Learn it together, and welcome honest discussion. And if you've been blowing it, we'll talk about how to handle that in the next chapter.

Godspeed, Game Master!

4

THE REPENTING PARENT
Give Me the Truth. Wait...No...Nevermind....

As a parent, I often feel like a failure. I see the model of Jesus, I study His Word, and I walk away thinking, "I have so very, very far to go."

Then, the enemy consistently jumps on my shoulder and reminds me of specific failures. He reminds me of the time when I spoke more harshly to my sons than I should have. He brings up the time I was grumpy with the whole family over something silly. He rehearses times I've been too busy and disengaged from my daughter. And he really enjoys reminding me of ways I have failed to set the right example.

If my kids were writing this chapter, they would shape their fingers and thumbs like the letter "L" and plant it squarely on the center of their forehead with delight. *Loser!* They *love* to do that to Mom and me—in jest, of course. Oh, but how often it is true! The longer I live, the more intimately aware I am of how many ways I am still a loser when it comes to being like Jesus. At least I'm a growing loser.

This is where the Christian home and the teen parent relationship become a true portrait—a living picture—of *grace.*

A Living Picture of Calvary

What does Jesus do when you fail?

He forgives. Based upon His death on the cross—His full payment for your sin—He extends mercy and grace. He loves unconditionally. He doesn't reject or revile. He *redeems.*

He doesn't ignore your sin—for it cost Him dearly—but He doesn't condemn you either. As with the woman caught in adultery, He doesn't condone your sin, but He doesn't throw stones either. To the man who acknowledges his sin, He simply says, *"Neither do I condemn thee: go, and sin no more"* (John 8:11).

To avail yourself of His measureless grace, eternal forgiveness, and undeserved mercy, you must simply acknowledge your sin. No hiding. No running. No cover up. No denial. No rationalization. Just face the truth. Acknowledge the sin, confess it, and forsake it. "Go, and sin no more." Repent.

What an amazing grace! What an amazing Father! This is the unconditional love and unmerited favor of our Saviour. This is His message to a failed human race. This is the central message of His Word. This is who Jesus is and what He does. This is His ministry of reconciliation. This is how big the cross of Christ really is!

And He has placed you, parent, into the ministry of reconciliation as well. *"And all things are of God, who hath reconciled us to himself by Jesus Christ, and hath given to us the ministry of reconciliation"* (2 Corinthians 5:18). God intends for your home to be a living portrait of Calvary played out every day in the eyes of your children. He expects your home to be a place where sin is neither rationalized or ignored, but where it is repented of and where reconciliation occurs regularly.

So here's the question of this chapter: *How big is the cross in your home?*

The Redemptive Process

Consider for a moment how the failures—both yours and your child's—if handled properly, can be a living picture of the Gospel every day in your home.

For reconciliation and redemption to occur, there must first be offense—"I have sinned."

Offense must be met with confrontation—"You have sinned. Failure has come between us. Our relationship is divided."

Confrontation should be answered with confession—"I know it was wrong and I want to make it right. I am sorry. Please forgive me."

Confession then meets grace—"You are forgiven."

And grace leads to restoration of the broken relationship—"Now that we are reconciled to one another, let's grow together to be more like Jesus."

Failure leads to *confrontation*, which leads to *confession*, which leads to *grace*, which leads to *forgiveness* and *growth*. This is how the Christian life works, and how the Christian home works.

If you are looking for a home where confrontation and sin don't happen, you will never find it. If you are looking for a book written by a flawless parent with a utopian home, it doesn't exist. If you are looking for a home that pictures God's grace on the cross, you can have that right now.

It's all about how you handle failure, sin, and offense—in your own life and then among the members of your family.

Reality Parenting

I had a cute but convicting conversation at my daughter's bedside one night before we prayed. It went something like this:

"Haylee, if you had to give me an A, B, C, D, or F as a daddy, tell me how you would grade me…"—she tried to interrupt, but I continued—"…in the area of *listening to you.*"

"A-plus," she said with a smile. (Didn't think I would do so good on that one.)

"How about in giving you my attention when you need it?"

This time she paused to think, "A-minus." (Twice, I was higher than expected.)

"What about in coming quickly enough when it's time to pray with you at night?"

Long hesitation, then a wry smile, "You want the *truth*?" (She was nine.)

"Yes, I want the complete truth…no matter what."

"Hmmm…maybe a B,"—hesitation again, then—"or *lower.*" (She giggled.)

I could tell she didn't want to hurt my feelings. "C-plus?" I asked.

"Or lower.…" (Insert another slight giggle here.) "Maybe just a C."

The conversation continued for several moments as we played this very important "game"—me inventing areas for her to grade, and her giving the *truth.* Fortunately, I passed, but I definitely walked away with some demerits and some things to work on.

In that moment, I gave Haylee permission to be gut-honest with me. And she gave me a moment to make some things right with her. We finished the "game" with knit hearts. I was forgiven, and she had fewer things bothering her about our relationship. More than that, she had the knowledge of how grace works—because she extended it to me. What a life lesson!

Our kids know where we fail and will forgive us—if we would have the courage to make them comfortable telling us the truth.

As we prayed, I promised her I would work on those things that were "less than an A." She smiled, we hugged, and she went to sleep. Then I thought, "Why haven't I asked my kids these questions more frequently?"

I'm not suggesting that we formulate our whole parenting philosophy on our children's bedtime opinion polls. But, let's face it, it's tough to nurture the heart if we don't have it!

Maybe we could call it *"reality parenting"*—knowing exactly where you stand with your kids. If I'm getting a failing grade with my children, I'd better work on *me* before I try to work on *them*!

Sometimes the truth hurts a bit, but it's always a helpful reality check. If we want our children to follow our God and own our values, we must begin by knowing where we stand with their hearts.

This practice also sets the stage for times when you must ask them to face their own failures. If they've seen you respond with repentance, they will be more likely to follow. If they've seen you lie, rationalize, defend, and make excuses...well, you get the point.

What to Do When You Blow It

Every Christian parent fails. This chapter isn't about failing less—though that's a great goal. It's about dealing biblically with failure. As you live out the Gospel before your children, I challenge you to swallow your pride and learn some simple phrases:

I'm sorry. I hurt you. I got angry with you. I neglected you. I ignored you. I made you feel less than loved and valuable. I reacted in my flesh rather than in the Spirit. I acknowledge that I sinned, and I'm truly sorry that I did.

I was wrong. I didn't get the whole story. I didn't see the big picture. I jumped to conclusions. I misunderstood your heart. I shouldn't have. I sinned. I dishonored God, and I reject my own behavior. I was wrong, and we both know it.

Will you forgive me? I acknowledge that my sin hurt you, and I need your forgiveness. I repent of my failure and desire to grow to be more like Jesus—so I'm asking you not to harbor this sin in your heart. Don't let this become a wedge between us. Don't become bitter or resentful toward me. Don't allow my flesh or failure to continue to be a problem between us. Please choose instead to forgive me.

I'm sorry; I was wrong; please forgive me.

Easy to read—tough to say. No words in all the English language are more difficult to utter. And no prideful or arrogant parent wants to say them. However, if you desire to truly have the heart of your teenager, you're going to be doing this plenty (at least if you're as big a loser as I am).

Parent, if we want our children to have the right relationship with Christ, we must model it through sincere, transparent humility. When you do wrong, and your kids see it or know about it, deal with it. When you offend your child or fly off the handle inappropriately, sit down and ask forgiveness and make it right. Prideful parenting is hypocritical. It shuts a child's heart to the things of God.

Repentance is healthy. It stops sin in its tracks. It prevents sin from festering and creating bitterness. Repentance brings reconciliation—between you and God, and between you and your child.

"Confess your faults one to another, and pray one for another, that ye may be healed. The effectual fervent prayer of a righteous man availeth much" (James 5:16).

"Have mercy upon me, O God, according to thy lovingkindness: according unto the multitude of thy tender mercies blot out my transgressions. Wash me throughly from mine iniquity, and cleanse me from my sin. For I acknowledge my transgressions: and my sin is ever before me. Against thee, thee only, have I sinned, and done this evil in thy sight: that thou mightest be justified when thou speakest, and be clear when thou judgest. Behold, I was shapen in iniquity; and in sin did my mother conceive me. Behold, thou desirest truth in the inward parts: and in the hidden part thou shalt make me to know wisdom. Purge me with hyssop, and I shall be clean: wash me, and I shall be whiter than snow. Make me to hear joy and gladness; that the bones which thou hast broken may rejoice. Hide thy face from my sins, and blot out all mine iniquities. Create in me a clean heart, O God; and renew a right spirit within me. Cast me not away from thy presence; and take not thy holy spirit from me. Restore unto me the joy of thy salvation; and uphold me with thy free spirit. Then will I teach transgressors thy ways; and sinners shall be converted unto thee" (Psalm 51:1–13).

Open Hearts, Open Conversation

Have you ever had an open conversation with your child when you asked, "How can I be a better parent?"

Have you ever sensed tension between you and your child and honestly, sincerely asked, "How have I offended you? How have I hurt you?"

Have you ever sensed relational or spiritual withdrawal and asked, "Do you have enough time with me? Is there a struggle that I can help you with right now? Do you feel close to me, and if not, why? What can I do to make it right?"

These are difficult conversations to have, and sometimes they take hours, but they are part of growing in Christ as a Christian family. It may take some time for your child to open up, and it must be a non-threatening atmosphere for that to happen, but it will change your relationship dramatically.

If there is a chance that you will blow up, become defensive, or ignite an argument, the questions won't work. This must be a completely transparent moment of humility and grace.

Think about it—for the rest of your child's life others will fail them and they will fail others. Where and when do they learn how to handle failure? How do they learn to respond to failure? What should they do with their own failures?

In the above portrait we see biblical repentance modeled at the parental level and lived out in the whole family. For you and your child, there's only one option regarding those who fail you. Forgive them, as Christ has forgiven you, and refuse to become bitter.

"And be ye kind one to another, tenderhearted, forgiving one another, even as God for Christ's sake hath forgiven you" (Ephesians 4:32).

Willing to Deal with My Own Sin

Sometimes we parents are wrong—not only in our parenting, but in other areas of our lives as well—and our kids see it and know it. We can live in sin. We can hide sin. We can have bad attitudes and bad habits. In parenting, we can jump to conclusions. We can misunderstand and overreact. We can panic and be easily frustrated. Sin is in us because it's in our flesh (Romans 7:20). We care for our kids, and whether out of fear or flesh, we don't always express that care rationally when under stress.

When you blow it, own it. Become a repenting parent, and lead your children to learn repentance. Think of it this way—what right do I have to be respected when I'm right, if I can't admit when I'm wrong?

There will be frequent issues between you and your teen, but those issues are neutralized if they are resolved. If left unresolved, they simply build up and hold the relationship hostage under powerful, repressed resentment. Eventually they become explosive and divisive, and everyone wonders "where did that come from?"

Constantly pursue resolution through repentance. Sometimes you will *do* the repenting. Other times you will lead your children to repent. And you'll find them much more willing to repent if they have seen it modeled well. That's what biblical authority does—it is authentic, even in the midst of failure.

How could I possibly deal with my child's sin if I'm not willing to deal with my own? How can I expect my children to repent and make things right, if I'm not modeling that process? If I cover my sin, my kids will cover theirs. If I live inconsistently, my kids will resent my faith and possibly eventually reject it, but if I lead them in repentance by *being* a repenting parent, the whole spiritual dynamic of my home changes. Rather than a faith *faked*, it becomes a *"faith unfeigned!"*

"When I call to remembrance the unfeigned faith that is in thee, which dwelt first in thy grandmother Lois, and thy mother Eunice; and I am persuaded that in thee also" (2 Timothy 1:5).

As we close this chapter, take a moment and ask God to examine your heart and life. *"Search me, O God, and know my heart: try me, and know my thoughts"* (Psalm 139:23). Ask God to examine your home and lifestyle. Is there open, known sin?

Consider your lifestyle: Is there drinking, cursing, gambling, pornography, carnal music, worldly entertainment, or sinful practices?

Consider your relationships: Are there angry tempers with yelling, cursing, fighting, and self-centeredness? Is your home a war zone of wounded hearts?

If so, then the first step to being the right parent is to repent of these things. Sin is destructive. The inconsistency of living in open, blatant sin, and then feigning faith on Sundays wreaks havoc on a young heart. Our kids will not passionately follow a God toward whom we are complacent. They will not play that game. They will only become disillusioned and walk away.

Be a repenting parent—repent before the Lord regarding sin in your own life or home, and repent before your children regarding wounds and offenses that exist between you.

The goal isn't a conflict-free home or relationships. The goal isn't sinless parenting. The goal is to picture God's grace in the home—to repent of sin and resolve the conflict immediately and frequently so that loving relationships with God and each other can be the norm.

I echo Haylee's words to me—"*Do you want the truth?*"

"*If we confess our sins, he is faithful and just to forgive us our sins, and to cleanse us from all unrighteousness*" (1 John 1:9).

5

THE PRAYING PARENT
Help! My Kids Are Teens, and I'm in Over My Head!

Probably the most universal experience of parenting teens is an overwhelming "AAAGGGHHH!!! I have no clue what I'm doing!"

Welcome to the fraternity of the fumbling and frustrated.

Not long ago, a panicked parent approached me about a difficult situation with a rebellious twenty-something "child." "What can we do?!" she asked. When my first answer was, "We can pray," the response was, *"That's all?!"*

If you're thinking that way—*stop. Now.* And keep reading.

This chapter is probably the most important of the whole book. But buckle up—it's also probably the hardest to practice.

"Something's going wrong in the heart of my child, and I'm not sure what to do!" Ever been there, parent? Have you ever seen the fruit of attitudes, behaviors, and decisions growing from the young branches of your child's life and been terrified by what's producing that fruit—what sinful root might be fueling a destructive direction? What do you do in these situations?

What do wise parents do when they don't know what to do?

It's easy to feel powerless, to feel like a parental failure, or to panic in overreaction. The simple fact is—parenting is one of the most overwhelming and daunting responsibilities that an adult can assume. To be responsible for the physical, emotional, relational, intellectual, and spiritual development and health of another soul is enough to drive any well-balanced adult into an asylum! It's scary because we know we're in over our heads. Too often, our parental panic is merely a subconscious reaction to the fact that we don't really know what we're doing.

Here's some great news for you. When you feel helpless, *you're not.* When you feel powerless, *you're not.* When you feel that you don't have the knowledge or expertise that parenting requires, you have access to the greatest Parent of all time. You have access to the timeless wisdom of Almighty God and His Spirit at work in your life. You have access to His guiding voice through His Word.

You and your child have instant access to the perfect Father, and He is supremely capable of helping you navigate difficult family circumstances. He is ready and waiting, in a split-second, to come to your side, give you wisdom, and help you understand deep issues of the heart and how to respond.

God's Promises about Prayer

Look at God's promises to us when we "call upon Him."

Psalm 50:15—*"And call upon me in the day of trouble: I will deliver thee, and thou shalt glorify me."*

Psalm 91:15—"*He shall call upon me, and I will answer him: I will be with him in trouble; I will deliver him, and honour him.*"

Psalm 145:18—"*The LORD is nigh unto all them that call upon him, to all that call upon him in truth.*"

The single most powerful parenting practice is simply prayer—calling upon God. And the most powerful expression of that practice is when you pray *with your children*. Does that sound simplistic? It isn't.

Yes, it's simple, but oh so difficult and complex. If you've tried recently to pray with your children or family, you know what I'm talking about. And I'm not referring to praying before a meal. I'm talking about coming together in a focused moment to talk to God and seek His help and guidance. No parenting effort will ever encounter as much spiritual resistance. No parenting exercise feels so awkward (at first), and no parenting practice is more powerful and transforming to the heart and to relationships.

When you pray with your children, you are doing the one thing Satan fears the most—and the one thing that most brings God's power and presence to bear in your situation.

So buckle up for some resistance. Prepare to press through some awkwardness.

How to Make It Happen

Let's investigate this a bit more with some practical steps to praying with your children:

Accept the responsibility of spiritual leadership. Dad, this begins with you. It begins with understanding that God has called you to shepherd your family—to lead your family spiritually. He expects you to be the initiator of walking with God and taking your family on that walk with you. If your family will grow spiritually, it should be with you leading the way.

Whether or not your dad did this is irrelevant. If you are in Christ, your Heavenly Father is your perfect role model now, and He will empower you and enable you to be what you need to be for your family. Believe it and embrace it. This is your reality now—accept it and move forward.

Decide on the best time to pray together. For many families this would be bedtime or the beginning of the day. There are some great reasons to end the day with your children in prayer. After a busy day, what could be better than opening our hearts together before God, placing the events of the day in His hands, and acknowledging His Lordship in our lives? What better way to fall off to sleep than having just spoken to our Heavenly Father together? What better way to say to your child, "I love you and cherish you as a gift from my Father" than to say it to the Lord in the presence of your child?

Pray together individually and as a family. There's something special about praying as a family—everybody taking a turn to speak to the Lord. But there's also something special about kneeling by your child's bed—one child at a time—and talking to God just the two of you.

It's impossible to continue in contention during these moments. Pride breaks down. Strong wills melt. Bad attitudes dissolve in the presence of Jesus. The most divided parent-child relationship cannot stay divided much longer when both commit to praying together on a daily basis. These are amazing, supernatural growing moments that nothing else can create.

Pray personally and transparently. Don't preach at or lecture your child through your prayer. Begin by thanking the Lord for all of His good blessings—especially your child. Confess out loud your love and commitment to this child. Thank the Lord for giving you this child and letting you be the parent of someone so amazing!

Then, pray for yourself. Confess that you need God's help to be a good parent. Ask for wisdom. Ask for guidance. Ask for help in leading this young life to love the Lord. "Lord, help this son/daughter to know how much I love them and You! Help me to be a good father...."

Finally, pray for your child. "Lord, give him strength tomorrow. Give him wisdom to do the right thing. Help her to walk with you, love you, and grow in your grace. Help her to have the strength to fight temptation. Give him the courage to talk with me if there is a struggle in his heart...."

Express physical affection during your prayer. Again, whether or not your parents were affectionate, or whether or not you are the "affectionate type" is irrelevant. Kids need our physical affection, so there can be no excuses here. Just be affectionate.

Hold them in your arms. Hug them. Put an arm around them. Hold their hand. Put your hand on their arm or neck. Put yourself in some sort of physical contact with your child as you pray. This communicates love and acceptance. And if your child responds in the same way, it communicates a tender, open heart toward you. Make this open, affectionate relationship your goal. If you don't share it now, pursue it until you do.

Be serious but not too serious. As we'll see later, kids like to laugh— and sometimes they even laugh when they pray. Somewhere between the land of high-church piety and utter blasphemy is a land of reality where people enjoy God and He enjoys them. I'm not saying be flippant, but don't be afraid to be respectfully light-hearted with your child in the presence of God. Let your kids know that they can enjoy Him and He enjoys them. He likes the sound of their laughter! And it's easy for kids to laugh when Dad is praying over dinner and says something like, "And

Lord, you know that Mom did her best on this dinner, but it's still going to need Your touch…please help it to taste good."

When they were little, my kids' favorite line from my prayers was, "And Lord, please help Mom to have a better attitude.…" That one always elicited a good solid round of giggles just before we began to eat. And thankfully, God always answered that prayer. Mom's attitude was always better almost immediately.

Visit for a few moments. Bedtime moments are critical moments. Make the most of them. Play around a bit. Tickle your younger children. Wrestle with your boys. Tell a story. Ask them how their day went. Express interest and attentiveness. And then, in the shadow of your Heavenly Father, and in the presence of your loving acceptance, let them drift off to sleep with good things on their mind.

As we wrap up this chapter, consider a few final observations about this most powerful parenting practice:

First, if this is new for you, it will be difficult at first, but will soon be natural. In our "flesh-against-the-Spirit" battle, this takes some time to feel natural. Press through that awkward stage, just like you did when you first dated your spouse. Like every other spiritual step, the foreign feel of this will dissipate in time, and it will become as natural as any other conversation.

Second, don't force your child to pray. If there is some relational distance or damage, or if this is a new discipline for you, your son or daughter may feel uncomfortable at first. Give them some space, and don't get frustrated. In time, if you accept their hesitation, they will come around. Your love for God and faith in Him will gradually develop their love for Him as well.

Third, understand that your child's heart was designed for this. Your child's heart was created for closeness with you, which should ultimately lead to closeness with the Heavenly Father. You are attractive to your child—knowing you, being accepted by you, being close to you matters to them. It's a craving of their soul. And so also is being close with God and knowing Jesus. Their hearts will blossom and thrive in His presence. It's up to you to lead them there.

Fourth, don't make this a marathon. We're not talking about an all-night prayer meeting here. It doesn't need to be long, but it does need to be sincere and genuine.

Fifth, this is tough. It requires time and sacrifice. It requires that you turn off the TV, even if a news story really has your attention. It requires that your spouse work with you as a team, reminding you, even nagging you if necessary. It requires courage, faith, commitment, and tenacity. It requires obedience to the promptings of the Holy Spirit to pray even when it's tough to pray.

Finally, pray *for* them more than you pray *with* them. Your children are never beyond the reach of your prayers. I challenge you to daily lift them up before the Lord. Pray that they will honor Him, love Him, seek Him, and obey Him. Pray that they will have courage and wisdom. Pray for their future spouse, their future decisions, and their preparation. Pray that God would give you wisdom and insight into their hearts and unique needs. There is nothing you can do that is more powerful than praying!

When You Reach Your Wits' End

Think of a moment recently when you were most at your wits' end in parenting. What did you do? What was your natural response? When you discovered your child did something that dishonored the Lord; when you received that call from the school office or when that parent approached you with difficult information—what did you do? When your child suddenly and openly defied you or rejected you—what did you do? When you had that frustrating confrontation between the two of you, what did you do? What will you do when that happens again?

Think of it this way. You can turn to your own limited understanding and perspective to pull together a human solution, which won't work. You can fight it out, wounding each other and escalating a conflict, until both hearts are hard and cold. You can panic, overreact, and later regret your carnal response. You can make a bad situation worse by ignoring God's desire to be involved and bring resolution and growth.

Or you can pray.

You can swallow hard, grab each other's hand, get on your knees, and invite Jesus to change your hearts and your situation. Only He can soften your spirits and resolve your conflict until both hearts—parent and child—are soft and close once again. Only He can give you wisdom and grace to rise above your natural, carnal responses and give you Spirit-filled, Christlike responses.

It's up to you.

Begin with Believing

Do you know where this all begins? It begins with *believing that it matters*—believing that prayer can make a difference.

Prayer is a simple act that packs nuclear spiritual power.

But if you don't believe that, you probably won't unpack that power. If you choose to ignore this powerful practice, you're doomed to continue a long string of recurring parenting mistakes. And you're leaving your child to themselves in discovering a personal, wonderful, amazing Heavenly Father.

Isn't it about time you unpacked the nuclear power of prayer in your family relationships? God's arms are open. His attention is yours. He loves to hear from you, and He loves to help parents and children nurture healthy relationships with Him and each other. Why don't you begin entering His presence with your child today?

"Call unto me, and I will answer thee, and shew thee great and mighty things, which thou knowest not" (Jeremiah 33:3).

6

THE COMMITTED PARENT
Romance Killers, Back Off!

Kids are killers—serial *romance* killers. They are obsessive-compulsive over it.

It's like they are wired with a sixth sense of when Dad and Mom might be attracted to each other. Little alarm bells go off in their heads. They knock on doors, call cell phones, pick fights, light fires—whatever it takes to kill the romance. They'll have none of that business going on. No sir!

They can even wake up on cue. It's like some sort of sick, preemptive sibling rivalry. "If I can prevent the conception of a sibling, I will have won for life! (Cue maniacal laughter.) Don't you even think about kissing that woman!"

It's wrong, I tell you. Just wrong.

Years ago, my wife and I came across a humorous poem. For obvious reasons, we both dislike it, but we laugh every time we read it:

Marriage at an Early Urge

Author Unknown

Nice night in June, stars shine, big moon

In park with girl, heart pound, head swirl

Me say love, she coo like dove

Me smart, me fast, me never let chance pass

Get hitched, me say, she say—Okay!!

Wedding bells, ring ring, honeymoon everything

Settle down, married life, happy man, happy wife

Another night in June, stars shine, big moon

Ain't happy no more, carry baby, walk floor

Wife mad, she stew, me mad, stew too

Life one big spat, nagging wife, bawling brat

Realize at last, me move too fast!

The Best Gift You Can Give Your Kids

The greatest single gift you could ever give your kids is a strong, committed marriage. And ironically, one of the greatest single threats to your marriage is children.

Yes, the very thing they seem to work the hardest at preventing (at times) is the thing they most need in the home—a happy, fulfilled, abundant, overflowing, passionate, committed, romance-filled, Christ-centered *marriage.*

"And said, For this cause shall a man leave father and mother, and shall cleave to his wife: and they twain shall be one flesh? Wherefore they are no more twain, but one flesh. What therefore God hath joined together, let not man put asunder" (Matthew 19:5–6).

"For this cause shall a man leave his father and mother, and shall be joined unto his wife, and they two shall be one flesh" (Ephesians 5:31).

A Strong Marriage

Makes you a better parent—two are better than one, and parenting was designed to be a team sport. A strong marriage fuels the home with bonded hearts. An unshakeable, loving relationship provides for a stable, secure family.

Makes you a present parent—you like to hang around someone you love. The more fiery the love, the more you want to be together. So, when your marriage is strong, you'll start making as many excuses as possible to be at home more. Tension-filled marriages have the reverse effect—we start inventing reasons to avoid home. Let me let you in on a little secret—a great marriage is a LOT more fun than career advancement!

Makes you a happier parent—a strong marriage fills your heart with delight. That delight overflows into every other relationship—especially your children. Kids love to hang around happy parents. Unhappy parents, on the other hand, they avoid like the plague.

Makes home a unified place—families are designed for unity, togetherness, and singleness of purpose. When Dad and Mom are one in heart, the whole home functions differently, for the better.

Makes a whole family the standard—modeling a strong marriage shows your kids that great marriages are still possible. The world is telling them otherwise. Make a biblical family the status quo for your kids.

Makes your kids want to stay married—kids who see happy marriages know they are worth the effort. When they see Dad and Mom working through things and staying committed and happy, they capture the vision—they dream of having the same. And when their marriage goes through tough stuff later in life, they will know that staying together is the best option for a life of real fulfillment.

If You Leave Your Family

During my twenty years as a student pastor, I wept with and counseled dozens of kids the day after a parent left home. These are among the most difficult moments of ministry. These hearts are the most devastated that I ever personally witness. The grief, the depth of loss, and the gravity of the wound is unspeakable.

If you have a broken home, I write these words not to shame or guilt you. I share them to prevent others from creating such senseless trauma. Consider with me for a moment what happens if you leave your family:

If you leave your family, …

- You rebel against and shame the name of your great God.
- You rebel against God's Word and clear commands.
- You rebel against God's design for marriage and family.
- You rebel against who God has called you to be in Christ.

If you leave your family, …

- You rob your wife or your husband of their hopes, dreams, health, future, stability, dignity, and a million other valuable treasures that mere words could never justly describe.
- You rob your kids of stability, home, unity, love, a million family memories, and a much longer list of spiritual blessings.
- You rob your Saviour of glory and a good testimony that should emanate from your life.
- You rob your friends and neighbors of a strong and shining testimony of the true Gospel and the power of God.
- You rob your future from the stronger marriage that would have resulted from working through tough stuff.
- You rob yourself of a clear conscience, pure heart, good name, and the respect of people who love you.

- You rob your church of a godly leader, a biblical model of family, and an example of strong commitment.
- You rob yourself of the opportunity to express courageous leadership through family trials.
- You rob your grandkids of the privilege of knowing their grandparents as a married couple.

If you leave your family, …

- You lose a lifetime of God's blessings and rewards for your faithfulness in marriage.
- You lose a lifetime of a clear conscience, trading it for a lifetime of guilt and regret.
- You lose the love you could have shared with someone who loved you when you were quite unlovable.
- You lose the privilege of having godly and respected influence in your children's lives during their adult years.
- You lose the joys of many years of family unity, precious times, treasured memories, and spiritual rewards.
- You lose opportunities to mentor others through difficult seasons of life.
- You lose your dignity as a faithful, respectable man or woman.
- You lose a list of valuable life blessings much longer than this chapter could contain.

If you leave your family, you rebel against your God and you rob others—which means they lose…and you lose…big time!

That's a lot to leave behind for a stupid bowl of stew—I mean, a bit of illicit pleasure or a delusional season of selfishness. It's not worth it. Not even close! *Don't do it.*

Beg God for help, get biblical counsel, hold on to your family, and refuse to ever let go! Work through it by God's grace, no matter how long it takes!

Leaving is NEVER worth it, and STAYING always is!

Whatever you do, don't leave! You will regret it!

BFFs

For our twentieth wedding anniversary, God allowed Dana and me to spend a few days on the central coast of California. In summary, it rained all week long, and we *loved* every moment together. God gave us an especially memorable afternoon of sunlight when we were able to walk along some ocean cliffs, enjoy the giant waves, watch the sunset, and savor the unspoiled coastline. It was one of the most memorable days of our married life. Little did I know that one year later, I would walk those same cliffs with the same woman—only this time my body would be sick with cancer and chemotherapy.

As we were looking at the photos of those trips recently, we were thanking God for His grace and patience with us. I leaned in toward her, smiled, and said, "You're my BFF!" (That's sixth grade girl talk for "Best Friends Forever"—and if you're a man, I do not recommend you use it in any normal context.) Then something caught my attention. All around our bedroom are mementos of twenty-two years of trips like this—little candles, sea shells, and keepsakes we've used to decorate our room to remind us of these special times when we went away to renew our marriage—somewhere far away from the "romance killers"!

At least once (and often twice) per year we have retreated together for a few days. Early in our marriage, we read somewhere that this was wise to do, and so we made it a priority. It has never been about spending a lot of money. It's usually just a short break. But oh, how valuable and blessed these times have been.

These trips must be important, because every time we've planned one, every possible interruption comes up to prevent it from happening. These retreats are never easy to make happen. We feel guilty for leaving the kids. We feel bad for being away from ministry. We wonder if it's the right time or if we can afford it. We wrestle with missing a basketball game or a church event. We nearly talk ourselves out of it every time.

But, in the end, *marriage wins.* Marriage gets the priority. Commitment wins. If our marriage stays strong, our kids win, our ministry wins, and everything else is better off.

Parent, do your teens a huge favor—send the "romance killers" away every now and then, and give them happily married parents. Make your marriage a priority. Say *no* to every reason not to, and just say *yes* to becoming and staying best friends.

When I married Dana, it wasn't because I needed a helpmeet, a cook, a housekeeper, or even a ministry companion. It wasn't so I could neglect her for most of our life together. *It was because I really, really liked her and liked being with her—and wanted to continue experiencing the relationship that God gave us!*

Statistics prove that most dating couples spend *far more* time together than married couples do. Personally, I'd like to die knowing that we defied that statistic. Don't let it happen to your marriage. It honors God to give your marriage plenty of time, and He makes up the difference in every other area.

All of life goes better—especially parenting—when your marriage is on solid ground and your spouse truly is your BFF!

Keeping Your Marriage Fresh

When we were engaged, there was one thing we dreaded—*someday becoming one of those married couples that appear to barely tolerate each other.*

You know—those couples who never even hold hands or exude joy in being together. We vowed to each other that we would do everything within our power to resist the trends and habits that take a couple gradually down the path to boredom, mediocrity, and relational monotony. Not even knowing what it would require, we vowed to each other to "keep the romance."

Here are some suggestions that could help you win more than you lose when it comes to renewing your marriage:

Spend time together: A good marriage takes lots and lots of TIME! You can't fast track a strong relationship.

Listen to each other: Value the sound of the other's voice. I meet some husbands who get tired of listening—don't do that. Be thankful that *you* are the one she's chosen to talk to! What a compliment to you. (See Song of Solomon 2:14.)

Bless and care for each other: Choose to find pleasure in taking care of each other. Delight in doing little things that bless the other. Those little things go a long way toward keeping love alive.

Retreat together regularly: These retreats will fuel your marriage and family in more ways than I could possibly describe.

Express physical affection: In many cases, the longer people are married, the less they touch. Be intentional about holding hands, sitting arm in arm, and snuggling up to each other. Life has its way of getting busy, and this one can easily fall by the wayside. Decide to remind each other when necessary.

Listen to good "marriage music" together: Build a collection of Christian songs that speak to biblical love and devotion. Let that music minister to your marriage.

Dream together: Look forward together. Whether you're planning a vacation or dreaming for the big picture and long term, unite your hearts behind shared vision. Common dreams will knit your hearts very close.

Read books that challenge you: Reading good Christian marriage books is like attending a well-prepared, truth-filled marriage retreat. They will refresh you, renew your love, and reset your focus on loving each other better.

Wait out the "weary places": Every relationship goes through valleys. Work pressures, financial pressures, busyness, and a myriad of other external factors can weigh down upon your marriage and bring you into a season of weariness. During these times you often lack emotional and spiritual energy, and your marriage relationship can be strained. Many couples "jump ship" during these times. Instead, look each other in the eye and say, "We will get through this…let's just be patient and keep holding on to God and each other."

Forgive each other quickly: Decide together that you won't hold grudges against each other. Expectations often lead to unmet expectations, which lead to disappointment, frustration, conflict, and distance. To keep your marriage fresh, you must be quick to own your failure and apologize. And you must be quick to forgive when you've been hurt or slighted.

Laugh and enjoy your family a lot: Every family has conflicts, but decide intentionally that you won't allow your family to be *dominated* by conflict. When conflict arises, work through it and resolve it, and then move back to the enjoyment mode.

Take walks together: Catch a summer evening sunset or take a late evening walk under the stars. Hold hands, take your time, talk, and enjoy the closeness with each other and with the Lord.

Well, this list isn't rocket science. It's pretty simple, but it works.

Standing United Against the Greater Enemy

One beautiful spring evening when our kids were still in elementary school, we decided to take a family walk together. The boys mounted their bikes, we placed Haylee into a wagon, and we all began our relaxing trek to the nearby Walmart where we intended to enjoy some ice cream.

A few moments into the trip, the boys were riding well ahead of us, and Dana and I began to discuss our upcoming family vacation options. Bad idea. I had one set of expectations, and she had another. And just a few moments into our talk, it became a "discussion"—you know one of those very "un-fun" ones. I wasn't seeing things her way, she wasn't seeing them my way, and so our friendly, family adventure became rather tense and frustrating. Haylee was too young to understand it, and the boys were oblivious to it.

A few blocks later, neither of us was enjoying the walk or winning the argument. But suddenly, something dramatically changed our perspective. Without warning, two vicious pit bull dogs came running around a corner and headed straight for our family. They were hungry. Seriously—they had napkins around their necks, and bottles of A-1 sauce in tow. They were ready for some fresh family meat!

Needless to say, our argument came to an abrupt halt as we were suddenly confronted with a very real and dangerous threat to our children.

The boys immediately panicked, and like little girls, ditched their bikes and ran wildly the other direction behind us—leaving me, Mom, and Haylee to be eaten alive. Yep, they totally freaked and had one thing in mind—saving their own hides.

As for me, I panicked too, but running wasn't an option. Haylee was the most vulnerable of the five of us, and I didn't have time to grab her *and* run *and* protect Dana at the same time. So, while my mind raced for possible options, I reacted with the only thing I could come up with on such short notice. It was weak, but I opted to stand in place, lift Haylee above my head, and let the dogs chew my knee caps off, while the rest of my family ran to safety. It was an instinctive response without much reason, and admittedly—stupid.

In a fraction of a second, I grabbed Haylee, lifted her over my head, and was about to shut my eyes, grit my teeth, and endure the crunching sounds when something unimaginable happened.

At this point, I should tell you, I had never heard the information I'm about to share. The appropriate response to a pit bull attack is to get angry, mean, and growl—barking louder and longer directly into the face of the pit bulls while baring your own teeth. The idea is to confront the animals with something meaner than themselves! In short—scare the snot out of them. (You should file this information for future reference.)

Now, my wife knew this. Somehow she had seen this on a Discovery Channel special—and to put it mildly, she took it seriously.

Suddenly, something more scary than the pit bulls came bounding from behind me directly into the face of the dogs. It was mean—super mean. It was growling, howling, barking, and baring teeth. It was jumping and pouncing—completely out of control. It was...*my wife!*

At this point, I'm standing wide-eyed, Haylee in the air, frozen in my tracks, watching my wife go ballistic—no—*NUCLEAR* on a couple of unsuspecting pit bulls. I'm telling you, these dogs picked the wrong woman on the wrong day! And then something even more unbelievable happened. The pit bulls started backpedaling, wide-eyed, and ran the opposite direction faster than our boys had! They met their match and gave up without even a hint of courage.

To make matters worse, the owner of the pit bulls rounded the corner just in time to see my wife freaking the dogs out and started yelling at my wife for scaring her dogs. Forgetting to switch out of pit bull mode, my wife simply turned and started screaming at the owner as strongly as she was barking at the dogs, "Yeah, well your dogs almost attacked my kids...." The owner then tucked tail and ran too!

Then, like someone flipped a switch, a calm settled over Dana. She turned toward me, stood up, straightened her clothing, and looked at me in a moment of rather uncomfortable silence. Our eyes locked.

There I am, still frozen, baby in the air, wondering if I'm about to be attacked by my wife. My first thoughts were, "Um…we can do whatever you want for vacation, Sweetheart!"

My first words were, "What in the world was *that*?!" (I was still hoping she wasn't about to pounce.)

And as calmly as you can imagine, she said matter of factly, "What? That's what you're supposed to do when you get attacked by a pit bull!" Like everybody in the universe knows this! In this moment, I still can't believe what I just witnessed. I married a werewolf and never knew it! But what a handy thing this is in the case of an unexpected pit bull confrontation.

Meanwhile, all the neighborhood was just staring out their windows saying, "Look at that guy's wife—she just saved his life! What a wimp."

Needless to say—I learned a lot that day. For one thing, I learned "Never mess with Dana!" She pretty much gets whatever she wants from that moment forward. But the greater lesson I learned was that our petty argument meant nothing in the face of a much more dangerous threat. A greater enemy called us instantly away from our selfish postures. Protecting our children called us to immediate unity and commitment.

That's why your kids need your marriage to be strong. There is a greater enemy bearing down on them quickly, and you are their first and most important line of defense. If the enemy can distract you, weaken you, and fracture you (as a marriage), then he will have a much greater success rate in ravaging your children.

What we need is more parents to go nuclear—to stand in the gap—to jump in between their kids and Satan. We need more parents to belligerently but prayerfully growl, "You can't have them! We stand committed and united in marriage to protect our kids—you're not getting to them through us!" God honors those kinds of passionate, committed parents.

Your kids need your strong marriage even more than my kids needed Dad and Mom to stop arguing and to engage in the battle for their protection.

Winning Against the Romance Killers

If you want proof that your teens are romance killers, here it is. I dare you to do it—you'll see that I'm right. Sometime when they're sitting around the family room, all into their stuff and unsuspecting—without warning just wrap your spouse up in a long embrace and start passionately kissing—right in front of them. Pretend you don't even see them sitting there. And watch what happens.

You'll think you've just walked into a cough drop testing facility. Gags, coughs, moans, groans, and protests will fill the air. They will go to pieces—just over a kiss. And the longer it lasts the louder they will protest. See—romance killers!

The fact that you live with teenage romance killers doesn't mean they have to win. Get committed, for a lifetime, to your marriage. Keep it strong. Keep it fresh. Keep it fiery and healthy. This truly is the greatest gift you can give your kids.

"Set me as a seal upon thine heart, as a seal upon thine arm: for love is strong as death; jealousy is cruel as the grave: the coals thereof are coals of fire, which hath a most vehement flame. Many waters cannot quench love, neither can the floods drown it…" (Song of Solomon 8:6–7).

Part Two
CLOSE
CONNECTIONS

7

THE ENGAGED PARENT
Learning from a Lazy Man and His Lewd Sons

"It's just a phase—he will grow out of it." "That's just what teenagers do—she'll mature." "All kids are this way—there's not really anything we can do to change that." "They have to be able to make decisions for themselves."

These and others are the statements we make to give ourselves permission to disengage as parents. Today's culture and the typical family tell us it's normal for kids to:

- Lock themselves up in their rooms.
- Avoid close relationships with parents.
- Have prolonged rebellion or bad attitudes.
- Act with immaturity and irresponsibility.
- Have little or no interest in biblical or godly things.
- Be sexually active before marriage.

Since we believe these behaviors are "normal," we disengage—we become *passive parents*. We essentially leave our kids to themselves to make their own mistakes and learn their own lessons. Sometimes we're tired. Sometimes we don't really know how to deal with an issue. Sometimes career or other interests distract us. Whatever the reason, passive parenting is *disastrous*.

A Passive Parent from the Bible

One of the best biblical illustrations of *passive parenting* is Eli, a priest of the Lord at Shiloh. His story is found in 1 Samuel 1–4, and the most outstanding statement about his parenting is 1 Samuel 3:13 when God said He would judge Eli's house because he failed to "restrain" his sons. Eli was fully aware that his sons were engaged in vile iniquity before God and the people, but he chose to do nothing. This response greatly displeased and dishonored God.

"For I have told him that I will judge his house for ever for the iniquity which he knoweth; because his sons made themselves vile, and he restrained them not" (1 Samuel 3:13).

The story is powerful. Eli was a large and indulgent man—somewhat lazy, and rather content with the status quo. He had two sons whom the Bible calls "sons of Belial"—God's way of saying they were wicked, ungodly men. They abused the work of God and His people. They perverted themselves and others. And they were living dishonestly and publicly shaming the name of God.

Eli's response was minimal. He talked passively with them a time or two, but took no other action. His inaction—his parental passivity—cost him and his family dearly. Let's examine Eli's passive parenting pitfalls and learn from his mistakes:

Passive parents defer parenting and spiritual development to institutions and environments. Though Eli brought up his sons in the service of the Lord, at the house of the Lord, they grew to despise God and His truth. Mere environmental changes—like church, school, or youth group—are no guarantees that our children will live honorably. Often, Christian parents choose to place their children in healthy spiritual environments only to disengage and expect the institution to take over. This just doesn't work. No pastor, youth pastor, teacher, or coach can replace or out-influence you.

This is especially easy for families serving in the ministry to do. After all, Eli could have rationalized "what better place to rear children than in the service of the Lord?" But parental neglect and passivity—even in a ministry context— always have disastrous consequences.

Engaged parents take personal responsibility to introduce their children personally to God. They fully engage in displaying a personal walk and a spiritual life, expecting healthy environments and supporting institutions to only *complement* what they are already teaching and modeling. Other influences and environments can support your godly parenting, but they cannot overcome your lack thereof.

Passive parents excuse their own sin and their children's sin. Eli basically rationalized his own sin as well as his sons'. He didn't want to change. He was *benefitting* from his sons' dishonesty. The only reason Eli even talked to them about their sin was that the people complained to him, not because they dishonored God.

Sometimes we tolerate sin in our children's lives because we don't want to give up our own. They know it, and we know it. In so doing, we dishonor God and passively endorse our children doing the same.

At times, we even respond out of embarrassment to our kids' sin. In other words, the only reason we engage is to minimize the disruption that our child's sin creates in our lives. Parents can have this attitude, "My child's struggle is embarrassing and inconveniencing me, so I need to get involved so someone can fix my child and I can get back to my life." This is a passive perspective, and our kids know it.

Passive parents avoid confrontation and responsibility. They see everyone else at fault—the teacher, the pastor, the youth pastor, the other kids, the church, the school, etc., but they don't see their own responsibility or the choices of their children at the root. Passive parents blame everyone and everything else but themselves or their own children. There's always another place to "point the spotlight."

Eli never really confronted his sons or took responsibility for his passivity or their sin. The Bible word *restrain* means to weaken or dim or diminish—like putting out a light. Eli should have removed his sons from influence and diminished their ability to carry on in their ways.

Refusing to deal with a problem is the worst response. Wise parents pay the price. They sacrifice. They go the extra mile. They will stay up as late as necessary, rearrange whatever is needed, take time off work, skip a meal, or make major changes in life to facilitate the need of a child. This kind of tough love speaks loudly to your teenager. It says, "I'm so committed to you, I will do whatever I have to do to make this right and help you through this." That's Christlike love, and it touches the heart deeply.

Wise parents don't defend or allow their children to blame others. They always support those who will help them biblically address problems, no matter how embarrassing a situation might be. Embarrassment is a small price to pay for the restoration of a life or the salvaging of a future.

Passive parents have the truth but don't apply it to their heart. They sit in church week after week, hearing (and sometimes presenting) the preaching of God's Word, but not really listening. Like pearls falling in the street, the truth is all around them, but it never penetrates the heart or impacts the lifestyle. The Word never leaves church *with* them. It never changes things at home.

Eli and his sons were *in the ministry*—surrounded by the truth on a daily basis, but it never penetrated the heart. There was a huge gap between God's truth and real life. What God *said* and how Eli *lived* were two very different things.

Wise parents always live with the ever-present reality of honoring God everywhere, all the time, in every way possible. It's not a church thing. It's not a Sunday thing. It's a *whole life* thing. It's a heart thing. Their Christian lives are 24/7, and living God's way is an ever-present reality.

Passive parents focus on behavior modification rather than heart transformation. They are more concerned with minimizing embarrassment than with truly molding the heart. Eli wasn't alarmed by the wickedness of his sons' hearts. He was just embarrassed by their behavior and the complaints he received. In other words, if their sins weren't so public and embarrassing, he wouldn't have been bothered at all.

Wise parents do not merely try to modify or manipulate outward behavior. They are always thinking of the heart and targeting heart transformation. They are always asking the question, "Is my child just conforming outwardly, or is his heart embracing God's truth?"

Behavior modification and outward conformity is a losing proposition. It's temporary and shallow. It always breaks down at some point, and passive parents are usually shocked and surprised when that happens. Our kids need deep, heart-level convictions built on the foundation of truth. They do not merely need to put on a show for the expectations of men.

Passive parents invest high energy into personal interests and career, but little energy into parenting. Eli somehow found time to serve God, but not time to restrain his sons, and God was not pleased. One of the saddest verses of the passage is 1 Samuel 2:25 when Eli is speaking with his sons and says, *"…if a man sin against the LORD, who shall intreat for him?…"* The word *intreat* means to pray for, intercede, intervene, or mediate. I believe *their father* should have intreated! Eli wouldn't even intercede before the Lord for his sons.

Later, when God pronounces judgment upon Eli's house, his response is rather ho-hum, *"…It is the LORD: let him do what seemeth him good"* (1 Samuel 3:18). What amazing resignation and passivity.

Wise parents fight passionately for their children. They intercede, they intervene, and they fully engage with their best energy and effort. They are willing to lose the world, but not their children. God honors those right priorities.

Passive parents ultimately resign themselves to "whatever will be." Eli never really invested much energy into trying to bring about a change. Perhaps he saw himself as the victim of circumstances and powerless in his sons' lives. That belief caused him to slump into fatherly resignation and neglect. I want to shout to Eli, "Get up and fight! Reconcile your relationship with your sons! Do something! Beg God! Plead for your family!"

Wise parents never give up, and they never believe it's too late to affect a change—even after many years. Many times I've seen faithful parents remain faithful through the struggles of a prodigal child for a long time. Through all the heartbreak, pain, embarrassment, and frustration, they never quit church, never left the Lord, and never stopped fighting. Rather than play a blame game, they just kept loving, praying, and living faithfully. Though their child was adrift, they remained the anchor. Many times, I've seen those children come back to the Lord and to their spiritual anchor—their prayer-warrior parents. One of those success stories is my own father who came back to the Lord as a young dad. Parent, it's never too late to see God work in the heart of your child. Don't ever give up.

Passive parents will answer to God for their own neglect, not their children's choices. God created free will. It was His idea. At the end of the day, our adult children have the power to make choices that we cannot control. God holds them responsible for those choices. Eli was not responsible for his sons' wickedness, but he was responsible for *knowing* about it and doing *nothing* (1 Samuel 3:13).

One of the greatest motivators to awaken us out of parental slumber should be the fact that we will be held accountable for our inaction.

What Do Engaged Parents Look Like?

Wise parents take all the opposite actions of Eli. They see parental engagement as *obedience* to God. They discipline and nurture their children, not merely to improve circumstances, control behavior, or minimize embarrassment. They do so because they *themselves* are obedient children of a Heavenly Father.

- Engaged parents view themselves as the most important influences in their child's heart.
- Engaged parents deal with their own sin before the Lord and then humbly lead their children to do the same.
- Engaged parents employ compassionate confrontation, and they take responsibility for their children.
- Engaged parents apply and live the truth seven days a week, not just on Sundays.

- Engaged parents target heart transformation, not just behavior modification.
- Engaged parents invest their best energy into marriage and family.
- Engaged parents never lose hope or give up in resignation.
- Engaged parents recognize their ultimate accountability to God as final authority.

Several years ago I had a conversation with a young lady in our singles department who was experiencing a marvelous time of growth in God's grace. Recently saved, she was literally basking in God's goodness and soaking up all the truth and wisdom that she could. It was wonderful to see.

But over the course of our talk, she expressed great disappointment in the fact that she's so late in learning many biblical truths that her parents should have taught her. How she wished they weren't *passive parents*.

How about *your* kids? When they are in their late twenties will they share the same disappointment? Or will you fully engage and nurture them by God's grace?

Learn the pitfalls of passive parenting from the story of Eli. Engage with energy and commitment. Target your child's heart with tenacity.

Engaging fully in the spiritual development of your children is nothing short of *honoring God*, and He responds quite favorably to that honor.

"...For them that honour me I will honour..." (1 Samuel 2:30).

8

THE PURSUING PARENT
Father Time Meets Desperate Hearts

One of the first questions I often ask a young person in a counseling session is simply this: On a scale from 1–10 (10 being the best), how would you rate your relationship with your parents? Then I ask the same question for each parent—Dad and Mom. Whatever the response, I then ask, "Was there a time when the number was higher?" If the answer is yes, I say, "What happened in your lives that made the number lower?" By this time, there are often tears forming in their eyes. And no matter the response, I then ask, "What would it take to make the number higher?"

There are many lessons learned from such conversations, but the one single take-away from all of them is simply this—every teenager deeply longs for a close relationship with Dad and Mom.

After spending many hours in such counseling sessions over the years, I can say with confidence—kids who spend quality time with their parents are very different from those who don't. They think differently.

They process life differently. They relate differently. They respond differently. They are less vulnerable, more stable, more courageous, more settled in their own identity, and more focused in their direction in life.

A healthy relationship with you is exceedingly important in your teenager's life. In light of this, wise parents are "pursuing parents"—they are in a relentless, passionate pursuit of a close-hearted relationship with their teenager.

"Only take heed to thyself, and keep thy soul diligently, lest thou forget the things which thine eyes have seen, and lest they depart from thy heart all the days of thy life: but teach them thy sons, and thy sons' sons" (Deuteronomy 4:9).

"And thou shalt teach them diligently unto thy children, and shalt talk of them when thou sittest in thine house, and when thou walkest by the way, and when thou liest down, and when thou risest up" (Deuteronomy 6:7).

"And also all that generation were gathered unto their fathers: and there arose another generation after them, which knew not the LORD, *nor yet the works which he had done for Israel"* (Judges 2:10).

Father Time

As our kids become teenagers in today's society, there is no doubt that our lives become busier on every level. The busyness impacts everyone in the family. For dad, it hits with bigger bills, more financial stress, more work responsibilities, and a more demanding schedule (especially for commuters). For moms, it is a more demanding home life, more home/work balance struggles, more schedule demands with the kids, busier school life, etc. For the kids, it is music lessons, sports practices, games, orthodontist appointments, science projects, Facebook, and youth activities. And we all know that this is the short list.

The results of this "potentially good stuff" can be devastating for a family who allows the schedule to take over. It is not exactly a hostile takeover—it is more like a gradual infiltration. Little by little our "together time" gets overrun by other important or entertaining things. The terrible results of this lost time usually take months and sometimes years to see. Eventually, the whole family is stressed, fragmented, distant, and depleted. We even start to feel like we just "don't get along." Many families just chalk this up as "normal." It is what happens when our kids become teenagers.

Wrong way to think.

This is not a teen thing. This is a father thing, and it can be overcome. Your kids need you, Dad—badly. They were created with a need for time with you—"father time."

(As a side note, it's important to say that, while the focus of this chapter is challenging fathers to be engaged in the lives of their children, these thoughts apply equally to both parents or single parents.)

It seems that the most critical battle of my ministry to families relates to getting fathers to spend time with their teenagers. Many appointments I have had with fathers in the past ten years start out talking about a struggling teenager—a son who is rebellious or a daughter who is distant. Without fail, eventually the father says something like this—"I haven't been able to spend much time with him since he became a teenager" or "She's closer to her mother than she is to me." The reasons for the problem always seem so powerful and compelling.

Dad, you are essential to your teenager's spiritual and emotional well-being. I fully understand the pressure of making the business successful, keeping the boss happy, and keeping food on the table; but if we are neglecting our kids in the process, we are dishonoring the Lord. This is counter-productive, since He is the one who promises to meet our needs in the first place. We work hard to make ends meet, to cover our bases, and to provide a better life: and as we do—we dishonor God by neglecting our children, which ultimately means the ends do not meet, bases are not covered, and life is not better.

In Haggai, the children of Israel were struggling with such mismanaged priorities. They were commissioned by God to rebuild the temple—His house. This was to be their priority, and He promised to be with them and provide for them. Yet, along the journey they got things "out of whack" and began making their own survival their primary goal. God's priorities took a back seat to their own agendas. And, as is always the case when we don't live by God's priorities, things went quickly down hill from there. Here's how God described it:

"Now therefore thus saith the LORD *of hosts; Consider your ways. Ye have sown much, and bring in little; ye eat, but ye have not enough; ye drink, but ye are not filled with drink; ye clothe you, but there is none warm; and he that earneth wages earneth wages to put it into a bag with holes. Thus saith the* LORD *of hosts; Consider your ways"* (Haggai 1:5–7).

No matter how hard they worked, they never had enough—they never got caught up—because they were dishonoring God in their priorities. On the other hand, as soon as they fixed their priorities, God's promises kicked in, and He provided for their needs. It all worked out when they simply honored God first. You can read about how God came through in the book of Ezra. It's a pretty amazing story.

The take-away is this: when you make healthy family relationships a priority, you are honoring God. When family life is whole, God is pleased, and He will help you cover all the other bases and meet the other needs. But when you neglect family for advancement in other areas, you are walking a dangerous and destructive path.

Turning Your Heart Toward Your Teen

Look at Luke 1:17 as it speaks of John the Baptist: *"And he shall go before him in the spirit and power of Elias, to turn the hearts of the fathers to the children...."* The word *turn* in this verse means "to revert or to turn about"—implying that the fathers' hearts are turned away from the children. The word *hearts* refers to "the thoughts and feelings." In other words, it was a part of John the Baptist's mission to turn the thoughts and feelings of fathers back to the needs of their children.

This single truth speaks of God's priority on "father time." It shows that your kids need more than physical provision. They need time with you.

So, how is the "father time" in your family? Are you working too much? Are you sitting in front of the TV more than in front of your teenager? Are you absorbed in other hobbies and interests to the detriment of close-knit hearts? In your child's life, nothing can replace the value of time spent with you. A Christian school, a church, a youth group—these things are wonderful gifts from God, but none of them can be what *you* can be.

Dad—please understand, this drift happens to all of us, but we must consciously choose to resist the trend and take a different path. Like breathing, sleeping, and eating—time with your children must be non-negotiable. Everything else in life should line up behind your God and your family.

This is a weekly discipline—not monthly or annually. Every week (or nearly so), your children need time and focus from you. It's not about spending a lot of money or finding entertainment. It is about being together—talking, connecting, laughing, and relating.

To put it as powerfully as I can—*I do not know of a problem that a teenager faces that cannot be fixed with the right kind of "father time."*

You are critical in every way to your teenager's spiritual and emotional stability and maturity.

Perhaps the scariest thing is this: we are all running out of time. They will not be teenagers for long. In just a few years, you will have all the time you need to work more, commute longer, and watch the news. For right now, give your kids what they need most—"father time"!

What Quality Time Together Looks Like

Let's dig a little deeper and ask, "What exactly does this time look like, and how much is needed to maintain a healthy relationship?" Let's get specific about what kind of time we're talking about.

Here are a few suggestions on how to have quality father time:

It should be one-on-one. I'm not saying you shouldn't have time with the whole family together, but you must complement it with one-on-one time with each of your children.

It should be frequent. If you haven't noticed, relationships can't be measured and meted out like a cooking recipe. They are *dynamic*— growing and changing. They never stay the same, and it's hard to give a formula that works perfectly every time. They are also *organic*—like a plant that needs nurture and attention to stay healthy. Without fresh water and attention, a young plant starts to dry and shrivel up.

This one-on-one time should be frequent. I suggest that you use a one-week period of time as your measuring stick. Plan your family life one week at a time, and determine to give each child some one-on-one time every week. And when you miss a week, the next week becomes all that more important.

It should be focused. This is not the time to watch TV together, stick the earbuds in, or be on the cell phone. Beware of this pseudo-father time. This is the time to talk, to relate, to laugh, and to interact. It's time to ask questions that generate response and reveal your teenager's heart. Only focused time can help you do that.

It should be Holy Spirit led. This is vital. The Holy Spirit knows exactly what's happening in your teenager's heart, and He can lead and guide you in the conversation. If you're distracted, this conversation will never happen the way the Lord would lead. Ask the Holy Spirit to give you wisdom and to give your teenager openness as you spend time together. Seek to serve and minister to your child during this together time.

It should be threat-free. This is not the time for parental lectures or discipline. To be sure, there is a time for that, but this isn't it. There's a big difference between parental nurture and parental lecture. The only way to have a heart connection and strong relationship with your teenager is to balance your "discipline time" with a different environment altogether. This should be a time when your teenager can open up and talk without the threat of you digressing into lecture mode.

My pastor, Paul Chappell, has often said in regard to these situations, "Accusations harden the will, but questions stimulate the conscience." Lead the conversation with questions that help you see into your teenager's world.

It should be flexible. Sometimes this weekly time together could be an hour. Other times it should be two or three. And on occasion, it should be a whole day or more. Your teenager needs a balanced variety of time with you. Have you ever taken your son or daughter away, just the two of you, for a whole day? If not, get it on the calendar—it's time.

It could involve serving the Lord and others. Some of the best time I've ever had with my children involved serving the Lord together. Go make a visit, share the Gospel, or deliver a gift together. These things and more will help your teenager enjoy you and enjoy serving the Lord with you.

It should be fun and funny. Have you noticed that teenagers like to have fun? At the same time, have you noticed that we as adults often take ourselves and life too seriously? One of the great delights of parenting teenagers in my home has been their sense of humor. They keep us laughing constantly. Find some wholesome things you can laugh at together. Do what they enjoy. Make memories that they will cherish. Few things bond two hearts like shared laughter and enjoyment.

It should sometimes be resolution oriented. On occasion, you will need to schedule this time simply to restore your relationship and make it right. In every home, the devil brings conflict and contention, but godly parents and wise fathers will not allow that conflict to go unresolved. Sometimes you'll use this time just to say "I just sense there's something wrong between us. How have I hurt you or how have I pushed you away?" You'll be surprised at where this conversation might lead. Reconciliation is a wonderful thing.

It should be need-driven. How often you do this and how long you spend together will be determined by the Holy Spirit's leading in your heart and your spouse's heart. My wife always knows better than I do about how much time our kids really need with me. She has a better reading of the emotional gauges of their hearts. She can always tell when they're running close to empty, which hopefully is rarely. The goal isn't to keep them barely above empty. The goal should be to keep them full! Seek the Lord's leading in how often and how much, and when in doubt, do more than you think is necessary.

It should be consistent. This is a key. Spending lots of money on a once-a-year vacation or getaway isn't nearly as beneficial as a few hours each week. I'm all for vacations and family getaways, but I'm *more for* consistent, day-by-day relationships that nurture the needs of the heart one week at a time. Without this, our kids will resent us and resent whatever takes us away from them. If you serve in ministry and are neglecting your children, you're simply setting your kids up to resent the ministry and ultimately God.

A lot of kids walk away from God after high school. Often, that rebellion is rooted in resentment toward parents. Though it is wrong, in *their* minds it is justified. Why would they want a relationship with your God if their relationship with you is nearly non-existent? Time together is critical in that process of helping them develop a genuine heart for God.

Overcoming the Heart-Vacuum

Have you ever noticed how some teenagers (or adults for that matter) seem so passionately drawn into certain things—friendships, dating relationships, music, lifestyles—to the point that they become obsessions?

Have you ever known a teen (or adult) who didn't seem quite as susceptible to these forces? On one hand, you have a teen who is "addicted"—who would rather die than lose a friendship or a cell phone. On the other, you have a kid who could seemingly take it or leave it—they just have a healthy balance about life. What's the difference?

Often we judge this obsessive behavior as something that all teens experience. Perhaps that is true on some level, but the types of clingy, passionate obsessions I often see are anything but normal. They more closely resemble a starving refugee scavenging for food. It's amazing how a starving person will eat just about anything to stay alive, isn't it?

Let me try to paint a picture for you. Imagine that your child's heart is like a plastic container submerged underwater. The container represents the heart; the water represents the world and all the corruption that Satan wants to put into the heart. The air in the container represents healthy spiritual things—a strong relationship with parents, the Word of God, godly authorities, etc.

Now, since no heart is completely or perfectly sealed from the world, let's poke a few holes in the container in our mental image. What starts to happen? Immediately the air begins to leave the container and escape to the surface, and the water begins to enter.

It's a simple vacuum effect. The container cannot contain a vacuum. It's scientifically impossible. To remove air without allowing water in would lead to only one result—total collapse.

Now, if our goal was to keep the water out of the container (in spite of the holes) there's only one solution—keep the air flowing in the container. So, let's stick a straw into the container and start blowing with all of our might. As long as we're forcing more air into the container, the water will be withheld. Yet the moment we stop forcing air in, the vacuum effect takes over, allowing water back in.

Let's apply this. Why are young, Christian hearts sometimes attracted to bad things—obsessive friendships, godless media, and carnal culture? Among many reasons, a part of this relates to a relational/spiritual/emotional vacuum in the heart. In the absence of "good air," the heart is more and more susceptible to the water of the world.

"Good air"—healthy home relationships and influences—must be supplied intentionally and regularly. I'm talking about good input like quality family time, one-on-one with parents, good music, wholesome entertainment, etc. Where this "air" is escaping or missing altogether, you will always find a desperate teen grasping spiritually and emotionally for anything (or anyone) to fill the heart—anything to avoid a collapse.

Satan is only too ready to fill your teen's heart with the filth of the world. The moment you allow a parental vacuum, you can expect your teen's struggles to grow progressively worse. Our kids become more desperate for friendships, music, dating relationships, etc. when their hearts are longing to be filled. The already strong suction of the world's filth is only increased by the lack of "fresh air" at home.

If this is happening in your teen's heart, you must immediately start filling that heart with "good air" as you also seek to remove the bad water. Start immediately overdosing on time together, prayer together, good input in the home, and quality family time. Rebuild that missing closeness that the heart craves.

At the same time, plug some holes. Look for the areas where you might be allowing "water" in. Maybe you will stop listening to certain music, stop watching certain TV shows, or follow the Holy Spirit in some other area in purifying your home life. In the short term your teen may fight you. But eventually (and it may take time) your "healthy-hearted" teen will return. Fresh air will make a difference.

So, watch out for the "vacuum effect" in your family. If your teen is showing signs of spiritual drowning, look to the heart. Don't waste all your time on the fruit problems—go to the root. Focus on the needs of the heart, and begin filling that heart with good input and healthy home relationships. See the longing for what it really is—a longing for "fresh air."

Your teens need you now more than ever in their lives. They need you to pursue a healthy relationship with them. So, be a regular breath of fresh air—and by God's grace, keep breathing!

"Keep thy heart with all diligence; for out of it are the issues of life" (Proverbs 4:23).

9

THE ENCOURAGING PARENT
Somebody Say Something Nice to Me!

"When you're a teenager, you're always in trouble...." She was speaking as a recent graduate of our youth group and was trying to give me a little insight as to how most teenagers feel. I thought I would put her theory to the test. A week or so later, in front of a gathering of several hundred teenagers I asked this question, "How many of you feel like someone is always on your case—like you're always in trouble?"

Now, be mindful, this was in a group of decent kids—most of them had good attitudes and sincere hearts. Never have I seen such immediate and unanimous response from teenagers. Every single hand went straight up into the air on cue!

I must say, while we all laughed briefly, my heart sorrowed in that moment. I was staring into the faces of some of the greatest Christian teenagers I've ever met and yet they apparently *felt* like failures. These kids dress right, live right, give, share the Gospel, serve Jesus, and love the

Lord. They are the "cream of the crop," and yet when asked directly, they *felt* like blots on society.

Let's put ourselves in their shoes for a moment. Let's say you're fifteen years old. By now, there is solid, scientific proof that your brain is 50–65% into a process of tearing itself apart and rebuilding itself one cell at a time—so your gray matter (dying brain cells) is at an all-time high.

In addition to this your body has radically changed in the past two years. Your feet are twice the size they were, your braces have added a new dimension to your identity crisis, your complexion is in full bloom, your life is far busier and more demanding than it has ever been (in other words, you're not watching Nick Jr. and peeling Crayolas any more!), you are highly insecure about who you are in the eyes of others, and you are learning more about life than your half-adult brain can possibly assimilate.

To top it all off, the whole world seems to notice every single thing you do wrong—immediately—and proceeds to jump on your case and verbally beat you to a pulp for it.

Now, I'm not excusing sin or saying we should lighten up on dealing with problems—that's all a part of being a biblical authority. But honestly, I wouldn't want that life again for anything in the world. Would you?

Growing up through the teen years, while wonderful, fun, and memorable—to some degree it was just flat painful. I don't know too many people who would love to be that insecure, that awkward, and that "in trouble" again.

Do you remember the power of positive words to your heart when you were that age? Can you say, "*Fresh water to a thirsty POW*"?

When someone came along and told you what you were doing right or recognized something good—it was like wind beneath the wings of an eagle—fresh strength, renewed desire, courage to press on. I remember those positive words. Fortunately, God gifted me during those years with parents, pastors, and loving mentors who shared encouraging words often. How about your teenager?

Most teens generally feel inundated with rebukes and are starving for encouragement. They feel that everything they do even minutely wrong is in the spotlight, yet the things they do right are overlooked and even unnoticed. We adults are too good at picking out the wrong and quickly correcting it, but we expect the right, and therefore we barely notice it. In fact, we often completely disregard the learning, the spirit, and the effort that "doing right" required. How sad. We so easily allow those gigantic spiritual victories to slip by unrecognized.

God's Word says in Proverbs 25:11, *"A word fitly spoken is like apples of gold in pictures of silver."* Take that verse and make it a central part of your relationship with your children. Of course they will mess up. Of course they will fail. Of course they need your correction. But far more than that, they need to hear when they got it right. They need an encouraging relationship with you.

They need our applause, our smiles, our pat on the back. They need to hear, "Son, I'm really proud of you and here's why…!" They need a note detailing all the things we noticed that they did right. They need our prayers rehearsing all the good things we see in them. They need a personal lunch, eye to eye, when you look deep into their hearts (past all the gray matter of the brain) and say, "You are such an exceptional person and here's why…." Are you giving these things?

The teens I spend time with are generally getting life right. They are headed in the right direction, growing in God's grace. But more often than not, they *feel* like they are failing. That's a sad disparity. Sometimes we can blame the devil for discouraging them. But sometimes we must point the finger squarely at ourselves for not acclaiming the good. If you want to motivate your teenager from the heart to do the right thing, praise him, applaud her. Tell them how proud you are of the good that you see. Fan the flames of spiritual living.

Ten to One

How often do young people need affirmation? Try this formula: *ten to one*. Try saying ten positive things for every one reproof or rebuke. Don't stop your loving, firm correction, but offset it with ten affirming, encouraging statements. And when you need to rebuke—begin and end it with something positive and encouraging.

Join me in a quest to change the perception of the younger generation.

How motivated would you be to live right if you felt that God never noticed and it really didn't matter?

Fourteen Ways to Affirm Your Kids

Not long ago, one of my sons asked my wife, "Was dad proud?" Then he said, "I work hard to make that man proud!"

His statement reminded me of the power of parental affirmation… and of how often I fail to let my kids know that I am proud of them. Affirmation is huge! The most hopeless young person is the one who feels he or she "just can't win." And, too often, we as parents inadvertently lead our kids to that conclusion.

I want to wrap up this short chapter with a list of suggestions. I'm not the "affirming parent" that I want to be—and that's partially why I made this list. But these are the things that I see passionate parents do well. These are the things I respect in successful parents who I'm trying to follow. So, as food for thought, here's a starter list of fifteen ways we could affirm our kids this week:

Just say it. Pause in an unexpected moment and say, "Hey, I just want you to know I love you, I'm proud of you, and here are some reasons why!" or "Hey, I want you to know you're really doing a great job in (fill in the blank here)!" For instance, just randomly thank your son or daughter for their excellent attitude. (When they have one, of course!)

Write a specific note to them. Write out the good qualities and successes you see unfolding in their lives. Even better—mail it to them. Their surprise is well worth the fifty cents!

Speak highly of them in front of others. When they can hear you, speak up to others about some of the ways you see them growing, doing right, or working hard. They will rise in their attempt to live up to your description.

Acknowledge their hearts and intentions. It's easy to judge only the outcomes and ignore the intentions. Let them know you understand their good intentions, even when the outcome isn't what was intended. The fastest way to deeply wound the heart is to pounce on undesirable outcomes and fail to appreciate pure intentions.

Seek to understand their emotions. There's something powerful about having "the way you feel" validated by someone in authority— even if the circumstances can't change. You may not be able to give them their way, but you could let them know you understand how they feel.

Reward them tangibly. Give a gift for no reason other than the fact that you were thinking of them or you are pleased with their good efforts or growth in some area.

Honor them intangibly. Prefer them in a way that lets them know they are highly valued and esteemed by you. Treat them like you would treat someone very important in your world.

Spend time with them. They already know you're busy, so giving them quantity and quality time will speak loudly regarding your love and honor toward them.

Express physical affection. Just randomly pause, wrap them up in your arms, and squeeze for a while. And while you do, say something like, "I love you so much! I can't believe how awesome you are!" I recently heard a Dad say to his teen daughter, "When you were little, you used to be cute and cool—what happened?" Then he paused, winked and continued, "Now you're beautiful and really cool!" The look on the young lady's face was priceless.

Surprise them. Their favorite restaurant or meal, a new book, a special event, or a spontaneous family memory—do something memorable that they aren't expecting, and let them know it's because you are proud of them.

Do a random act of kindness. Help them clean out their closet, fill their car with gas, send a quick text message, or pick them up at school and go to lunch. There are about ten million other ideas you could come up with on your own.

Genuinely admire them. Pause, think about your child, and consider the ways they excel. Consider the areas in which you might even envy them—and then celebrate those qualities. (Be honest—sometimes and in some ways our kids flat put us to shame.)

Defer to their decision or preference (when possible). Don't fight battles that are worth losing. Sometimes there's a lot more to win by losing. Preferring one another is a wonderful expression of love, and it's very biblical. For instance, let them choose where or what to eat for dinner. A truly miserable family is one in which everyone is bent on fighting for their own way.

Make a big deal of good decisions. When your kids make a wise choice, go nuts! Celebrate spiritual victories with all the zeal and energy of a lunatic Super Bowl fan. When possible, let them make a key decision and praise them for "getting it right."

As I write this, I long to grow in this area. I have so much room for improvement—perhaps you do too. This is one area where our intentions are often masked by a harsher reality and behavior. Ask the Lord to give you an affirming spirit, and purpose to make encouragement a consistent and abundant part of your parenting efforts.

Encouraging words are, to your teenager, what fresh, cold water is to a dehydrated POW. Your positive words minister grace to your teenager's heart. Why not sit down right now, grab a blank piece of paper, and reach out to your precious POW with some refreshing drops of affirmation?

"A man hath joy by the answer of his mouth: and a word spoken in due season, how good is it!" (Proverbs 15:23).

"Let no corrupt communication proceed out of your mouth, but that which is good to the use of edifying, that it may minister grace unto the hearers" (Ephesians 4:29).

10

THE LAUGHING PARENT
Being Weird, Growing Teeth, and
Other Strange Behavior

Once a year, we load up the family minivan and begin our family trek to Northern California for Thanksgiving. We've made this trip twenty times now, so we've gone from "middle-of the-night-driving" with kids in diapers to "middle-of-the-day-driving" with kids watching Buzz Lightyear to evening driving with teenagers playfully making jokes about us and each other. During a recent trip, the traffic was unusually heavy, which gave us several more hours of laughter on the trip together.

As you might imagine, five relatively witty people cooped up in a minivan for eight hours can get pretty funny. As my kids have grown, it seems they have inherited their grandfathers' and great-grandfathers' wits all at once. There are three of them—Lance (our twenty-one-year-old, who works hard at having an "all-together" image, but eventually ends up cracking up at himself the most), Larry (our eighteen-year-old and the funniest human being I know who sees humor in just about anything and always makes us laugh hard), and Haylee (our twelve-year-old going on twenty-five who often surprises us with her quick and insightful comebacks).

Our family never has more fun than when we're lovingly and playfully laughing at each other. Perhaps we are all half insane, I'm not sure. But once we get started, it seems there's no end. And the great part is, *no one* is exempt. By the time we're done, every single person in the family has had their turn in the hot seat for the enjoyment of the other four.

Imagine four people laughing their heads off and one moaning, "Nuh uh…" for several moments. Then without warning, it's someone else's turn. It's all in a spirit of "laughing at ourselves" with good natured, family spirit.

When the traffic finally cleared, we made our way to a café for dinner. It was early into dinner that Larry and I jokingly started putting little pieces of paper (from straws and napkins) into each others drink—like two kindergartners. I started it—me first, then him, then me again, then him—each piece getting a little bigger. He thought he "won" when he finally put an entire crumpled straw paper into my soda. He sat back in his chair with a self-satisfied grin as if to say, "Top that!"

This was when I grabbed my silverware (still tightly wrapped in a large napkin) and jammed the whole thing down into his drink. His jaw dropped, eyes widened, and the whole table started laughing very hard. It took us several moments to catch our breath. I had won, and he knew it. And the waitress never did understand what was really happening.

After some time of laughing ourselves silly, we finally quieted to catch our breath. Everybody had enjoyed laughing with and at one another. In a few quiet moments of driving, I began to contemplate the nature of the family fun we had enjoyed. Is there a method to the madness? Of course there is. Proverbs 15:13 and 15 teach that a merry heart is a "continual feast" and produces a "cheerful countenance."

Learning to laugh together (and often at ourselves) is a huge part of family life. Being able to take the good-natured laughter of others helps us grow thicker emotional skin. And being able to join in the laughter *at ourselves* helps us keep a proper perspective. We all tend to take ourselves too seriously. All families tend to have rivalry. We compete with each other unnecessarily. But families that learn how to laugh together have something pretty special.

It was shortly after I shared these thoughts with our kids that Haylee started talking. Incidentally, at the time she had about four teeth that were only partially grown in. Suddenly, picking up the playful teasing once again, Larry looked at her and said, "Haylee, why don't you stop talking and just grow some teeth." (But she was talking and missed it.) So, being proud of Larry for coming up with a "great one," I repeated it to her. She stopped mid-sentence, smiled with a cute frown, huffed a little, and instantly shot back to me—"Well, why don't you stop talking and just grow some hair!"

At this point, the whole family absolutely fell apart with laughter. My wife laughed the hardest. I too laughed. Haylee? She just gloated. She was so proud of herself. Yes, of all the great one-liners of the trip—this was the *very best*. Too bad it came at my expense! It was almost like there was an unspoken crowning ceremony—an invisible awarding of a gold medal. We all knew no one would top that one.

And once again Dad was getting a taste of his own medicine and having to apply his own lesson. Laughter is a wonderful gift! Being able to laugh at yourself is a great gift to others. Everybody likes to laugh, and everybody likes someone who can laugh at themselves—because when you get right down to it—we're all pretty weird!

Boundaries for Laughing Together

As you develop a spirit of laughter and humor in your family, I encourage you to protect some basic boundaries:

Boundary #1: Laugh at yourself first. Start with your own weirdness and embrace it.

I recently came through a battle with cancer. As difficult as that time was for our entire family, that season actually provided a lot of laughter in our home. For the better part of ten months I was not in my right mind much of the time and that brought about a lot of funny moments.

One of our favorite recurring moments of hilarity is when we sit down to play a game called "Bible Outburst." In sixty-second increments, each team is required to answer a list based upon a Bible question. For some reason, my wife is especially gifted at completely rewriting the Bible and causing the entire family to fall into laughing hysteria in her sixty-second answers.

In a recent game she actually had Eve selling fruit in the garden of Eden and Noah's ark coming to rest on Mount Arafat.

Boundary #2: Laugh at me only when *I'm* laughing at me. The easiest way to offend a family member is to begin laughing at them when they aren't willing or able to laugh at themselves. That's sacred ground—don't go there.

Boundary #3: If I struggle to laugh at me, help me get over it first—then we can all laugh. There's a Spirit-led dynamic to it, but it's fun to help a child begin to be able to laugh at themselves. It's fun to see God bring about those breakthrough moments when pride dies and joy returns.

Boundary #4: When in doubt, let's just all laugh at you (Dad)—If you're unsure, play it safe and lead the family in laughing at you (or Mom if she can take it). In time, your child's insecurity will dissipate as they learn from your example. It's not worth wounding a growing heart.

Laughing at the Right Stuff

Laughter at the right things at the right time does something wonderful and spiritual to align the emotions with God's stabilizing grace. The world is producing the kind of comedy that is undeniably and extremely displeasing to God. This is *not* the kind of laughter I am talking about. Sitting in front of a television and laughing at sexual innuendo is not healthy or honoring to the Lord.

God's Word is clear on this: *"Finally, brethren, whatsoever things are true, whatsoever things are honest, whatsoever things are just, whatsoever things are pure, whatsoever things are lovely, whatsoever things are of good report; if there be any virtue, and if there be any praise, think on these things"* (Philippians 4:8).

Your home and time together with your teen should be filled with laughter—good, God-honoring, having-a-good-time-together laughter.

One final word of caution, if your family doesn't regularly practice that strange behavior of laughing at each other—I wouldn't recommend that you just start randomly flinging insults around the Thanksgiving table. You might get yourself killed or seriously maimed by a meat fork.

Start with yourself, and make sure everybody knows they have the right to laugh at you first.

In closing, I would share that famous cliché, "The family that laughs together stays together," but it doesn't rhyme.

"A merry heart maketh a cheerful countenance: but by sorrow of the heart the spirit is broken" (Proverbs 15:13).

"All the days of the afflicted are evil: but he that is of a merry heart hath a continual feast" (Proverbs 15:15).

"A merry heart doeth good like a medicine: but a broken spirit drieth the bones" (Proverbs 17:22).

Part Three
GUARDED
HEARTS

11

THE INSIGHTFUL PARENT
You Know More than You Think You Do...

Do you understand your children? Do you know how to interpret their behavior? Do you see and understand early warning signs of future problems? Do you connect their outward behavior with the condition and direction of their heart?

God desires to help you find answers to these questions. He has called you to a position of understanding and insight. And your kids need your insight. Let's explore the possibilities of growing, by God's grace, in parental insight.

In Hebrews 5:12–14 we read a challenge to believers to be skillful in the Word and discernment:

"For when for the time ye ought to be teachers, ye have need that one teach you again which be the first principles of the oracles of God; and are become such as have need of milk, and not of strong meat. For every one that useth milk is unskilful in the word of righteousness: for he is a babe. But

strong meat belongeth to them that are of full age, even those who by reason of use have their senses exercised to discern both good and evil."

The word *discern* speaks of "judicial estimation"—it is wisdom, insight, and accurate perspective. This ability is something we should desire in every area of life but especially with nurturing our children. Many parents appear to only care that their kids stay out of trouble. But discerning parents see beneath the surface and seek to understand what's going on in the heart. Why?

Why the Heart Is the Focus

The heart is where biblical values are formed. Understanding the heart is the only way to know if your teenager's faith is representative of an authentic relationship with God or merely an outward, temporary show.

The heart is where questions are contemplated. Every child has questions, and when parents are out of touch, Satan is good at exploiting these questions and providing false answers with faulty conclusions. Insightful parents unearth those questions so they can provide biblical answers. (John 8:32, *"And ye shall know the truth, and the truth shall make you free."*)

The heart is where real relationships are cultivated. Like the root system of a tree or a healthy plant, it's beneath the surface—face to face, eye to eye, and heart to heart—that a strong relationship and authentic closeness are established.

The heart is where the spiritual battle is fought. The devil is going after our kids' hearts. He wants their emotions, their beliefs, and their attitudes. If we're going to win the spiritual battle, it must be fought at the heart level.

A discerning parent is constantly on a sacred pursuit of their child's heart.

Keys to Developing Parental Discernment

Let's examine ten contributors to developing parental discernment with our children:

Study and understand God's Word. The primary way that any of us grow in discernment is through the Word of God. The principles of God's Word provide a foundation for all parental thinking and decision-making. If you desire to become a discerning parent, you must become a student of God's Word and of good parenting books that expound God's Word.

Ask for God's wisdom. This is one of God's great promises given to us in James 1—that He will give wisdom to anyone who will ask in faith. Wisdom is the ability to see the real needs and know how to respond. It is the ability to see your family as God sees and to respond as He would.

"If any of you lack wisdom, let him ask of God, that giveth to all men liberally, and upbraideth not; and it shall be given him. But let him ask in faith, nothing wavering. For he that wavereth is like a wave of the sea driven with the wind and tossed. For let not that man think that he shall receive any thing of the Lord" (James 1:5–7).

Think of wisdom as "God's perspective." Why do you need it? Without it, you can't see the heart. You can't know or perceive what's really going on—which means you'll misdiagnose and mistreat issues on a regular basis. Like a doctor who doesn't have all the facts, you'll medicate problems that need major surgery and you'll try to perform major surgery on problems that only needed a Band-Aid and a baby aspirin.

There's always more to a situation than you can see, humanly speaking. Wisdom is what helps you, by God's grace, to see deeper—to see *through* a situation. It's one of God's greatest gifts to you, but it has two simple conditions:

Ask for it—how simple! Every day, and in every circumstance, just call upon God and ask Him for wisdom. But, here's the second condition...

Believe that He will answer—God says in verses 6 and 7, if you ask but don't believe, count on *not* having it. If you *ask* and *believe*, it's a done deal—guaranteed.

Pray with and for your children. Nothing will help you understand the heart like prayer. God answers prayer. God meets with you when you pray. God is present and involved in situations and circumstances where He is included through prayer.

Accept and obey the Holy Spirit's promptings. God gives every Christian parent an internal warning system—call it intuition, call it His still small voice, call it His peace or lack of it. It's real, and it's essential that you listen to it.

We can choose to accept or deny those warnings. They are easily reasoned away or ignored, but they are a most vital aspect of parenting. The times I have neglected these warnings, I have eventually come to regret it. The times I have heeded them, I have always discovered something that needed parental intervention.

Insightful parents accept God's internal promptings, even if they don't fully understand them or can't explain them. You don't need to explain what God is putting on your heart. You just need to heed and obey it.

There is nothing wrong with saying to your child, "I'm listening to God on this one, and He's not giving me peace. We just need to wait on Him and obey."

Be a team player with your spouse. God often works differently in the heart of husband and wife—to the intent that we cooperate and labor together in the grace of parenting. Think and talk about your children together with your spouse. Pray for them together.

When talking together, God will give you collective insight and the wisdom to create a biblical approach to dealing with the situations your children face. In these talks, Dad and Mom should mutually benefit from each other's perspective. When parents are a team, they heed each other's cautions, listen to each other's insight, and respond with unified hearts. This is a great gift to any child.

Spend quantity time with your children. Discernment takes study, and study takes extended time together. The more time you spend with your children, the better you will understand their ups and downs, their growth, and their behavior. Time with them will help you be able to sort through what is a normal part of their personality, what is a spiritual struggle, and what is the expression of a spiritual need.

As we said in chapter 8, this time should be *connected time* when you are communicating—not TV or movie time, and not time shared with other friends. Try to spend one-on-one time with each child each week. You may miss some weeks, but if *every week* is your goal, you stand a good chance of staying on course most of the time.

Choose to look beyond the surface. Don't focus merely on behavior. Ask where the behavior is coming from. Consider the reasoning, the logic, and the emotions that produce your child's decisions and behavior. This is discernment in action—seeing beneath the surface. For instance, when your child is misbehaving, obviously it's a sin problem, but ask the Lord, "What's the trigger?"

Connect the fruit to the root, and then address the root. You could spend forever picking bad fruit off of errant limbs, but it will keep coming back and getting worse unless you deal with the root. Heal the root, and change the fruit. As you dig beneath the surface, you venture into unknown territory—you lose your illusion of control, and you might fear what you will find. All that aside, you must pursue the root. You must know truth—what's really going on. And you must work at making your teenager comfortable with revealing their struggles rather than hiding them. This takes a lot of patience, time, prayer, and compassion.

As I write these words, I'm feeling healthier than I have in three years. Many years of chest congestion is gone. My persistent cough is nonexistent. Why? Because I stopped treating symptoms and discovered a serious hidden illness. Cancer was growing throughout my chest for at least eighteen months before it was discovered. To me it was just congestion and swollen lymph nodes—the stuff of infections like bronchitis. And so, cough syrup and antibiotics were staple parts of my diet—like a sixth food group.

Finally, a CT scan revealed what we really didn't want to know, but we truly needed to know. From that revelation, we were finally able to kill what would have been a *killer* problem.

You always need to know what's going on beneath the surface—for only then can you apply God's truth for lasting transformation.

Respond with biblical principles. Target the heart and pursue the transformation of the heart. Teach and transfer biblical principles and be ever sensitive to whether the heart is open to those principles or whether there is merely outward conformity.

Always point your child to the highest authority—the Heavenly Father. If you're not sure what to say or how to say it, then get help and seek advice. At all costs, point your child to God's truth as the answer for every problem in life. Always show them how your discipline connects to God and His ultimate authority.

Respond with appropriate authority. A variety of behaviors requires a variety of responses. As parents, we can't answer everything with a heavy hammer. Strong discipline should be but one of many tools in your parental toolbox. It doesn't make sense to kill a mosquito with an atomic bomb, but many parents use the atomic bomb for everything. That's unwise.

Ask the Lord to guide your responses and to make them appropriate to the need. Sometimes our children need reproof, other times rebuke, and other times exhortation. (2 Timothy 4:2, "...*reprove, rebuke, exhort with all longsuffering and doctrine.*")

Respond with compassion. No matter how firmly you deal with a situation, always rest your parenting on the firm foundation of compassion. Begin and end with compassionate nurture, even if firmness is needed in between.

If your child will hug you, pray with you, or respond to you, then the heart is open. If not, then the heart is closed. Whatever you do, don't rest until your child's heart is open to you.

You Know More than You Think You Know

Can I finish this chapter with a personal encouragement to you? You really do know more than you think you know.

It is no mistake that *you* are your child's parent. You are truly God's gift to your children. You were custom designed by God for their needs, their heart, and their development. You have been equipped in providential ways to be the parent that your kids need.

You don't need to compare yourself to other parents. Your teens don't need another kid's parents, and you don't need another set of kids. God brought you together by His eternal design, and it's just right. You fit together perfectly—though in reading this, you may feel that "the fit" has been damaged somewhere along the way.

You really are the right parent for your children, and you *know* what to do. You know how to pray, how to love, how to encourage, how to empathize. You know how to seek the Holy Spirit and ask God for wisdom, and He has promised to answer that prayer. He will guide you in those moments and help you say the right things. A part of this is simply believing God, stepping up with courage, and trusting Him to help you.

Finally, there's a lot more to learn. I challenge you to become a student of biblical parenting. Our kids deserve growing parents.

Other than the Holy Spirit, my best teacher on my growing journey in understanding my children has been my wife. Dana is the most discerning parent I know. God has given her a tremendous sense of our children's needs and the direction of their hearts. She has been my best parenting counselor. Many times, she has seen needs to which I was blind, and suggested a course of action that proved effective. It has been our constant commitment to stay united as a parenting team.

We're still in the middle of our parenting journey, and we are enjoying every moment of it. One thing is for sure—every child is uniquely special by God's design. That uniqueness should compel us to constantly rely upon the leading of the Holy Spirit in the moment-by-moment details of parenting.

Give your best effort to becoming an insightful parent by God's grace and power. Constantly ask Him for wisdom and guidance. He will answer, and your kids will thank you one day.

Don't you *love* parenting? What life work could we possibly do that has any greater value?

12

THE NURTURING PARENT
Speak Up, I'm Commanded to Hear You

If you had to quantify your ministry or parenting focus with the following words, which two would be the most accurate?

Managing Behavior or

Mentoring Hearts

It's easy to default to the "managing behavior" position. Why? Because managing behavior is easier. It simply requires a strong hand of authority and a list of expected behaviors. It's also more visibly rewarding—you can point to "how good" everybody looks and behaves. The scary thing is behavior changes when you're not around to manage it. And if you have teens, you won't be around for much longer. The countdown has begun, and the launch sequence has been initiated. Soon enough, your kids will be on their own, entering adult life.

Uh-oh—that's where merely managing behavior becomes a horrible waste of life and an utterly futile philosophy of family. Managing behavior is like babysitting—it's only concerned with the short term. It doesn't successfully transfer the ways of Christ to another life.

"Mentoring hearts"—this is the philosophy of family that creates wonderful, long-term fruit. But mentoring the heart takes time, training, teaching, investment, and sacrifice. It requires that you *practice* the truth, and make the truth *practical—or practice-able*. It's much more difficult, less immediately visible, less measurable, and less tangible than managing behavior. The results take longer, but they last a lifetime.

A portion of our parental efforts needs to be focused on managing behavior, but we shouldn't stop there. Behavior should never be our only gauge of success. Good behavior can be the product of one of two things—either it's the product of a right heart or the product of a stealthy heart. Good behavior can be feigned or unfeigned (2 Timothy 1:5). We must get below the surface and work to establish right beliefs which will ultimately drive right behavior.

Short-view parenting builds behavior. Long-view parenting builds belief.

If you wish to grow real faith in young lives for the long term, you must focus on nurturing the heart. Young people see through *behaviorism*. They learn the game. They learn how to keep everybody "off their backs." They go through the motions. They mistake "the motions" for the real Christian life, and eventually they walk away from the game because that's all it is—motions.

In so doing, they never truly fall in love with God, and that's the greatest commandment—love God with your whole heart. The Christian life, as family life, is all about relationships. Right relationships allow for the growth of right beliefs which will produce right behavior. It all flows in that order—"I love you unconditionally so I can teach you to believe biblically so you will behave honorably before Jesus Christ."

Relationships cultivate beliefs which bear the fruit of behavior.

You can produce behavior by force—parental legislation—but that doesn't last. It's like stapling fruit onto a tree branch. Eventually you'll just have rancid fruit. It looks good for a while, but it's artificial and short-lived. On the other hand, when right relationships nurture biblical beliefs, your child's behavior is driven by the heart, not by the heavy-hand. Genuine, biblical behavior will flow from an authentic root system of truth by the power of the Holy Spirit.

To put it simply, when you truly catch a glimpse of Jesus, you want to know Him. Once you get to know Him, you like Him and love Him. And once you like Him and love Him (and know He feels the same toward you), you usually don't want to run from Him.

What Is Nurture?

In a parent appointment years ago, a desperate mom stopped me in mid-sentence and said, "I'm sorry for interrupting, but you keep using a word—*nurture*. Could you explain to me what that means? I don't know what you mean by *nurture*."

In that moment, it became clear to both of us why her adult children were struggling in their relationships with God and their parents. There had been plenty of authority and legislation in their home for many years. There were lots of biblical rules and penalties in place. But there was little relationship, and even less biblical nurture. (The good news is it wasn't too late, even for adult children, and those adult kids today love God and their parents.)

"And, ye fathers, provoke not your children to wrath: but bring them up in the nurture and admonition of the Lord" (Ephesians 6:4).

The word *nurture* refers to the whole process of training, teaching, educating, and cultivating the life of a child. It includes the care and development of the mind, the morals, and the body; and it involves both proactive teaching and training as well as correction and chastening. For the context of this chapter, we're primarily talking about teaching and training.

What Does Nurture Look Like?

If we will embrace our responsibility to teach (nurture) and then keep our eyes and ears open, God will create plenty of opportunities for us to do so. Our kids' curiosity will naturally open doors for us to step through in training.

On a breakfast date recently, my daughter Haylee asked me, "Why did you choose to like Mommy instead of another girl?"

Wow! What a cool question! This was a wide open door for nurture—a golden opportunity to teach—to paint a portrait in her young mind of what qualities are truly, deeply attractive to a committed Christian man.

At the very instant she asked the question, the Holy Spirit immediately began to prompt me to not miss this teaching moment. And so, asking for wisdom, I began the list, teaching her along the way:

She was godly—she loved the Lord, walked with Him, and had a very good testimony with her friends and family. She wasn't worldly in her dress, music, or lifestyle (Romans 12:1–2).

She honored her parents—she was very close to her daddy and loved her family. They were her best friends, and I never saw her disobey or dishonor her parents (Ephesians 6:1).

She obeyed her teachers—she had a submissive spirit to those who were her authorities at home, school, and church (Romans 13:1).

She was meek and quiet—just as God teaches that beauty should first be about a meek and quiet spirit, she wasn't always trying to be the center of attention. She didn't flirt with boys and try to be accepted by people (1 Peter 3:4).

She wasn't rebellious—she didn't have a reputation for breaking rules, defying authorities, or having a bad attitude like so many young ladies (1 Samuel 15:23).

Following this, we had a talk about what real beauty is and isn't, and why. We talked about how beauty should begin in the heart and how her outward appearance should first honor the Lord above all. Since then, we've had several really good conversations with about a dozen follow-up questions from her inquisitive mind. That single moment, along with a few other events that the Lord arranged that week, brought about some of the most significant conversations I've had with her as a father.

How often do we miss teaching moments with our kids? I know I do! We get busy. We're on our phones, answering emails, sending texts, processing information, and making plans—too often at the detriment of a precious pause when an innocent heart would have asked a searching question.

These moments are doors into their thinking, their reasoning, and their hearts. If we miss them or ignore them, our kids get the message—"I'm not interested in you." Then these moments go away, and our kids take their questions elsewhere and find deception rather than answers.

Be sure, parent, if they can't ask you, they will take their questions somewhere else—and they will get answers. But they probably won't be the answers you would want them to have.

You are the truth bearer for your children. They should hear it from you first. You are the authority—the source of authenticity and truth. Give them truth against which they can measure all the other false information that culture will throw their way.

How awesome would it be if we could capture every teaching opportunity and use these real life situations to drive vital biblical principles deep into the hearts of our children?

Do you have a daughter? Has it ever occurred to you that, if her relationship is good with you, she's going to want to know what made Mommy attractive to you, so she can be attractive to you as well? And in turn, she will want to be attractive to a godly man like you in her future. What a powerful picture of the development of a young girl's heart for her Heavenly Father, her father, and eventually her husband. (I sure love the way God put life together.)

As a result of recent conversations between me and Haylee, our hearts are closer. She's whole. She's at peace. She knows things are good between her and Daddy, and that just makes life better. I can even see it on her face when she looks at me. What power we hold as parents to bring our children's hearts into stability and rest.

God's Instructions on Nurture

It's so vital that we listen to the Holy Spirit and be aware of potential teaching moments. They don't have to be limited to formal family devotions—though they can be and should be. They can be all throughout the day and night, woven into regular conversation and everyday circumstances. They should flow naturally and unrehearsed. They should remind us of God's ever-present hand in every situation.

Here's how God said it in Deuteronomy chapter 6:

"And these words, which I command thee this day, shall be in thine heart: And thou shalt teach them diligently unto thy children, and shalt talk of them when thou sittest in thine house, and when thou walkest by the way, and when thou liest down, and when thou risest up. And thou shalt bind them for a sign upon thine hand, and they shall be as frontlets between thine eyes. And thou shalt write them upon the posts of thy house, and on thy gates. And it shall be, when the LORD thy God shall have brought thee into the land which he sware unto thy fathers, to Abraham, to Isaac, and to Jacob, to give thee great and goodly cities, which thou buildedst not, And houses full of all good things, which thou filledst not, and wells digged, which thou diggedst not, vineyards and olive trees, which thou plantedst not; when thou shalt have eaten and be full; Then beware lest thou forget the LORD, which brought thee forth out of the land of Egypt, from the house of bondage. Thou shalt fear the LORD thy God, and serve him, and shalt swear by his name. Ye shall not go after other gods, of the gods of the people which are round about you; (For the LORD thy God is a jealous God among you) lest the anger of the LORD thy God be kindled against thee, and destroy thee from off the face of the earth. Ye shall not tempt the LORD your God, as ye tempted him in Massah. Ye shall diligently keep the commandments of the LORD your God, and his testimonies, and his statutes, which he hath commanded thee. And thou shalt do that which is right and good in the sight of the LORD: that it may be well with thee, and that thou mayest go in and possess the good land which the LORD sware unto thy fathers..." (Deuteronomy 6:6–18).

Ask God to give you wisdom to nurture this week. Ask Him to help you see the teaching moments and to know what to say when they come around. Your heart and your child's heart will never be the same.

Proverbs teaches, *"My son, hear the instruction of thy father, and forsake not the law of thy mother"* (Proverbs 1:8).

It's sort of difficult for a son to *hear* instruction if Dad isn't *speaking* it. Remember: *Short-view parenting builds behavior. Long-view parenting builds belief.*

13

THE GUIDING PARENT
Infatuation, Emotions, and Other Flammable Things

Have you noticed that our culture is trying to awaken and enlarge the desires of our young people at younger and younger ages? Today's parents often find themselves caught between the better judgment of their conscience and the pressure of a corrupt culture. We wonder how to handle the fact that our son or daughter is experiencing attraction to the opposite gender.

Do we panic, pack up, and move to the Alaskan wilderness? In some ways, we want to. Or should we go to the other extreme and start matchmaking by the time they reach eighth grade? Some take this approach as well.

In this chapter, we will explore a balanced and principled approach to nurturing and guiding your teenager's heart through these powerful new emotions and into a happily married adult life.

Proverbs 4:23 says, *"Keep thy heart with all diligence; for out of it are the issues of life."* I share this verse because it is your teenager's heart that is at stake in this battle. Satan would like to turn their heart the wrong direction, enlarge and pervert their desires, and ultimately rob their purity. A wise parent will determine to set up a watch-guard over their teenager's heart regarding these new attractions.

While I'm not pro-dating for high school students, I'm also realistic enough to understand that God-given desires and attractions naturally awaken during the teen years. Kids are going to be attracted to each other, and there's nothing we can do to change that—nor would we want to.

If we overreact and try to "ban" all communication and contact, they respond by taking their attractions underground—hiding them from parents and sneaking around rules. If we lower the bar and drop our guard, then dangerous emotions and physical desires take over and become destructive.

I believe we should strike a careful, biblical balance—teaching and nurturing our kids in how to manage emotions and how to keep their friendships healthy and Christ-centered until the Lord intersects their paths with the right person at the right time.

Let's consider some guiding principles that will help us navigate these unfamiliar waters of teen attractions:

Be the authority. As the parent, you must set the ground rules for how relationships will be handled in your family. You must lay the boundaries and the consequences of both keeping and breaking the guidelines. Often we think of punishment when it comes to disobedience, but what about the reward for obedience? Explain the incentives of honoring your boundaries. Help your teenager know exactly what your expectations are and why, and then reward them for honoring those expectations.

Be an understanding friend. As you exercise authority, you must also remember what it was like to experience these emotions for the first time. Remember the mistakes you made and why. As much as you seek to set and enforce guidelines, also seek to understand the way your teenager is feeling. If they believe you don't care or understand the emotions, they will disconnect and disregard your opinions and boundaries. Influence is the key here. Your kids need to trust you.

Communicate clearly and openly. Open communication is vital in a teen/parent relationship. You must be able to talk openly about what you expect and why. Explain your reasons. Nurture them through the logic. Talk through biblical principles of sexual attraction, fornication, purity, and the temptations of youthful lusts. (More on this in the next chapter.)

Expect things to start changing in junior high. Your teen will naturally be attracted to the opposite sex. Don't try to stifle or dismiss that God-given attraction, but respond to it wisely. Don't react—respond. Don't be threatened by these changes, but don't ignore them either. Handle them seriously in your heart, but lightly on the surface. Have some lighthearted fun with your teenager, but also have frequent serious talks on the subject of relationships that please God.

Maintain a group spirit in all teen relationships. Teenagers who are attracted to each other do not need to be alone—*ever*. The devil will constantly try to isolate them and draw them into emotional dependence upon each other. Exclusivity is a breeding ground for emotional idolatry, and exclusive teen relationships have nowhere to go but *wrong*.

Help them build strong friendships of the same gender. The teen years are tumultuous socially. Never is a person more insecure and longing for acceptance than during the teen years. As you become "best friends" with your own kids, they will more naturally desire friendship with good influences. Their stable hearts (rooted in a relationship with you and the

Lord) will make them stronger against peer pressure, temptation, and bad influences. Teach them what kind of friendships are healthy, and help them make wise choices in this area.

Help maintain the right pace in a friendship. Teenagers want to grab attraction and run to exclusivity and isolation as quickly as they can. They need you to help set the pace in keeping things light and right. You are the "pace car" that keeps your teenager's emotions from crashing. You must slow it down and keep it simple. Hours on the phone, talking in a corner at church, endless text messaging, exclusivity from the family or group, lower grades, always wanting to be together—these are warning signs of a relationship moving too fast and in the wrong direction.

See the teen years as the lab and yourself as the instructor. The teen years are truly the laboratory in preparing for adult life—the last stop on the road to responsibility. This is your final opportunity to shape character, establish values, and nurture the heart before some very serious and long-term life decisions are made. This is the time to deliberately help your son or daughter to prepare for a life-long relationship in marriage.

Never rationalize permissive parenting by your past failures. Be the parent God calls you to be, regardless of what kind of young adult you were. Stay involved and engaged with your teen, and mentor them through every step of this process right up until marriage.

Encourage a "just friends" relationship philosophy until graduation from high school. If your young person isn't ready to be on the road to marriage, then there is no reason to get wrapped up in an exclusive or serious relationship.

Teen relationships trade preparation for pretend. At a time when young hearts should be focused on growth and preparation for a future marriage, a teen couple merely suspends preparation so they can pretend to be married *now*. In light of all this, encourage your teen to maintain healthy friendships with the opposite gender—light ones. Help them understand the danger of becoming too serious or exclusive too soon.

I co-wrote a book for teens with Mike Ray entitled *Just Friends* (available at strivingtogether.com). In these pages, we shared biblical principles and practical advice on teen relationships and how to navigate them. I recommend that you read it first, and then lead your teen to read it—and talk through it together.

Watch for three danger signs: isolation, extended time, and physical contact. With young people, these three areas always lead to problems, and two of the three are not necessary until after marriage. Only an engaged couple needs to spend large amounts of extended time together as they plan and prepare for their life-long relationship. Don't accept the standards of secular culture in these areas. Keep in mind that many TV shows, movies, and much secular music will further fuel the fire of the very youthful lusts from which we are commanded to flee (2 Timothy 2:22).

Be approachable and preemptive with instruction. One of the biggest mistakes parents make in teen relationships is that they are completely unapproachable—whether from fear, busyness, ignorance, or insecurity. Granted, these discussions are uncomfortable for both parent and teen, but decide that your teenager will hear biblical answers from you before the questions are even raised.

Teenagers desire well-reasoned, biblical mentoring. They appreciate knowing what the Bible says and how to apply it. That's not to say they won't fight temptation—but at least they will *fight* it, and with your help and coaching, they will have victory over it.

Be involved as a parent. Again, nothing can combat the world's influence in this area better than a strong relationship and open communication with Dad and Mom. A good relationship with *you* will help your teen be far less vulnerable to peer pressure and lustful temptation. Open communication, prayer together, and time together will knit their hearts to yours and bring you into the battle with them. They need you to partner with them in the fight for purity.

Don't push your teen to date. Some parents lean to this extreme. Rather than being uninvolved, they are "over the top" in a pushy way. This is not natural and it's not healthy. You can't afford to get caught up in the emotion of your teen's youthful attractions. You are the voice of reason and stability. You must remain objective and principle-centered. Yes, this may create tension between you and your teen at times, but tension that keeps your teenager from driving into a relational ditch is *good tension.*

Have a heart for your teen's feelings, help regulate them and manage them, but on the other hand, if there is no fire burning, don't bring out the matches and gasoline. In this picture, you're a fire marshal, not a pyro-technician.

Don't take a "break-up" lightly. If your teen does take on a closer "friendship," start preparing them for the moment that things will change. Don't take it lightly when one or the other chooses to move on to another "friend." This is one of the most emotionally traumatic experiences that a teenager can face, and you must help them through it. Processing and healing through the emotions takes time, but they will get through it.

Don't panic when your teen notices a boy or girl. After all, you did too when you were their age. It's a normal, God-given occurrence that needs to be carefully managed by loving, parental authority. Set the biblical standard for your home, and enforce the standard with commitment.

At the same time, love your teen, show understanding, build a relationship, and communicate complete acceptance. Your young person will respect and honor this approach—and one day, from the vantage point of a happy marriage, they will be forever grateful for your mentoring.

The Right Person at the Right Time

Several years ago, a young man from our youth group married a young lady whose father had left her when she was five years old. Her father was completely absent from her life. Rather than become bitter and angry, this young lady chose to claim God's grace. Rather than withdraw into a perpetual identity crisis, and retreat into her hurt world; she chose to be godly and grace-filled—following the example of a Christlike mother.

What a joy it was to watch her wed and finally place herself into the loving arms of a godly young man. During their wedding photos, through my own tears, I watched sixteen years of longing come flooding out in her overwhelming emotional expressions towards her husband. It was a wonderful, awesome, blessed experience! God graciously gave her the desire of her heart and the longing of her soul—after she chose to trust Him fully.

Remember these words: *"The Right Person at the Right Time."*

This is the goal! This is the reason you are praying, teaching, guiding, and preparing this young life—*for the right person at the right time.* The devil will do everything within his power to prevent your teen from reaching that point. Keep your eyes on the Lord and on that goal.

God will grant you wisdom and strength if you will trust Him and honor His Word.

"Train up a child in the way he should go" (Proverbs 22:6).

"Keep thy heart with all diligence; for out of it are the issues of life" (Proverbs 4:23).

14

THE UNCOMFORTABLE PARENT
Talking to Your Teen about Sex and Purity

A photographer for a national magazine was assigned to photograph a raging forest fire. Due to the smoke and emergency traffic, he was having a difficult time getting the pictures he wanted. In a frenzy, he called the office and asked them to charter a plane and a pilot at the local airport.

Moments later he received the message—"The plane will be waiting for you when you get there." Only a few minutes later, the small plane was warming up on the runway when he arrived. As he jumped in, trying to catch his breath, he said, "Let's go, let's go...." Time was critical.

Once in the air, he instructed the pilot to the correct side of the fire and asked him to bank in a specific manner for the photos. The pilot curiously responded, "Why do you want me to do that?"

"Because I'm the photographer—photographers take photos, that's what I do!"

At that point the pilot turned white and said, "You mean, you're not the instructor?"

When it comes to teaching your teen about sex—*you're the instructor.* It's vital that you accept the job because many others are applying for it. God gave you to your teen to help them understand God's creation, navigate sexual temptations, and prepare for a lifetime commitment in a passionate marriage.

Consider this: *everyone and everything else in the world is talking to your teenager about sex—except you.*

The world, the media, the Internet, their friends, their teachers, their driving instructors, their sex education classes—it's unimaginable. And the things they are being told are simply wrong and wicked. The enemy's strategy is to awaken your child early, misinform them, enlarge their desires, pervert them, and then lead them into fornication (sexual sin) before they know what's happened. You can be sure he has a target on their back, and the center of the target is their sexual purity!

Just step back and look at the message of culture. Consider the most prevalent message of mass media. Everywhere, all the time, the enemy is shouting: *Have sex—whenever, with whomever, however.* If the enemy can rob your child's purity, he can often turn that into serious, life-long damage that runs very deep.

Some Scary Statistics about Sex in Culture

Guttmacher Institute did a recent study on teen sexual health.

By age 15, 13% of teens have had a sexual relationship.

By age 19, 70% of teens have had a sexual relationship.

The average age for a first sexual relationship for boys and girls is 17.

Each year, almost 750,000 15–19 year old girls become pregnant.

Tv is saturated with sex. According to Kaiser Family Foundation, 70% of all TV shows today contain sexual content—five scenes per hour. This means the sexual scenes on TV since 1998 have doubled. During prime time hours, 8 in 10 shows include sexual content, averaging 5.9 sexual scenes per hour.

The American Psychological Association estimates that teenagers are exposed to 14,000 sexual references and innuendoes on TV a year.

In addition, with cable networks and extreme or reality TV there's a new generation of sexual content on TV that continually points to the weird, absurd, degenerate, and perverted forms of sexual references. Studies show that a huge percentage of the viewers of sexually explicit TV shows are elementary-age kids.

The music industry is saturated with performers promoting outright perversion, abuse, and profanity.

The message of the world is sex, sex, sex—perverted, casual, adulterous, whenever, with whomever, however. Sex is god.

The message of the Bible is that sex is good within God's original boundaries—a lifetime commitment in marriage between one woman and one man.

Unfortunately, many Christian parents view the biblical topic of sexuality as disgraceful. But God doesn't. He has much to say about this wonderful and blessed marital gift.

Why Parents Don't Talk to Teens about Sex

Most parents never speak to their kids about sex—even though we know we should, and our kids want and need us to. Why is this the case?

Non-communication—Some spouses don't even talk to each other about sex. Silence on this subject is the context of many homes. Bad practice.

Family culture—We're uncomfortable talking about this because our parents never did, and it's unfamiliar and awkward territory.

Misguided "Christian" values—We're taught as Christians that this subject is somehow shameful and shouldn't be spoken of at all. The Bible speaks of it plentifully.

False assumptions—We think "they already know what they need to know," never considering that they don't, and what they think they know is largely *wrong*.

Fear—We don't know what to say, how to say it, or when to say it; and the whole concept of having this conversation makes us break into hives.

Ignorance—We're naïve enough to think they aren't thinking about it. This is just wrong—way wrong.

Past guilt—We're guilty over our own promiscuous past and feel unqualified or hesitant to parent in this department. This is just a deception.

Indifference—We haven't decided to care about their future and their preparation for marriage. We plan to let them "just figure it out for themselves." This is a really bad idea.

Let's face it, this is uncomfortable for most Christian parents, but it's a lot less uncomfortable than the resulting sin from our silence. You have two basic choices. You're going to end up talking to your kids about sex sometime, in some context. It's much wiser to be preemptive, premeditated, and proactive. Having this talk and opening this can of worms now will greatly decrease the potential of you dealing with serious sexual sin at some point in their future.

The message of this chapter is simple but loud. I'm urgently pleading here: *Talk biblically to your kids about sex! It's your responsibility!* If you choose not to, be advised that your silence is opening many doors of danger and temptation, and your teen will be unprepared for those temptations.

The Two Great Protectors of Purity

There are two things that will serve as great protectors of your child's purity. Remember them diligently:

The first thing that protects purity is the truth. Jesus said, in John 8:32, *"And ye shall know the truth, and the truth shall make you free."* Kids need the truth in this area. They deserve the truth. The whole world is screaming lies into their minds all day every day, and those who know the truth are silent. On the *deceptive* side of the information flow, there is a constant flood of noise. On the *truthful* side of the information flow there is silence and hesitation. No wonder our teens are destroying their lives sexually.

In teaching teens about this matter, I use a pink $5 bill from a Monopoly game. Without showing the bill, I call a young man up to the platform and ask him if I can give him $5. Of course, the whole room of teens comes alive with this. The young man always says, "Yes!" and smiles.

That's when I pull out the pink bill. Instantly everybody moans and sighs with disappointment—especially the guy on the platform. With surprise, I ask, "Why are you all disappointed?"

They are disappointed because they know the bill is fake. But digging deeper—how do they know that? Because they know what a real $5 bill looks like. They know the *truth*. And the truth makes them free—

free from deception, free from hurt, free from ignorance and all the bad results of living in darkness. In the light of truth, fakes are easy to spot.

This is how biblical truth works in the heart of your teenager. Apart from truth, they cannot discern the lies or spot the fakes. It all looks good. It all looks "consumable" and enjoyable. But under the spotlight of truth, deception is easy to see. I could never convince those kids that a pink bill is real—because they know what a real one looks like.

Similarly, if your children know what real love, biblical sex, honorable romance, and lifetime commitment really look like, they can easily spot and resist the lies. If they understand the whole picture, the long-term benefits of purity, and the subtle lies of youthful lusts, they will have the right information with which to resist and flee.

"Flee also youthful lusts: but follow righteousness, faith, charity, peace, with them that call on the Lord out of a pure heart" (2 Timothy 2:22).

"Dearly beloved, I beseech you as strangers and pilgrims, abstain from fleshly lusts, which war against the soul" (1 Peter 2:11).

The second thing that protects purity is approachable parents. Here's the agreement you need to make with your kids: "You can ask me *anything, anytime* about sexual matters, and I will give you a biblical, transparent and truthful answer." (*gulp!*) Yep, I mean it.

Would you rather they ask *someone else?* Would you rather they *Google* it? They *will* seek answers. They *will* find answers—wrong ones. You need to swallow hard and be the *answer machine*—a truthful, transparent one, not a vague, coughing, red-faced, embarrassed, "um… we'll talk about it when you're older" one.

Is this tough? At first, yes. Is it embarrassing? A little bit—but get over it, there are bigger fish to fry. Your teen will take you up on this offer because teens want to know the truth. Your son or daughter will approach you at the most unexpected of moments and say, "Hey, can I ask you a question?" It will be an open question. It will make you and your spouse want to "blush" and run for cover. On a few occasions, my wife has just turned red and said, "Um, I think I need to check the oven…" as she quickly attempts to dismiss herself (all of us knowing full well that she isn't cooking anything).

But think about this for a moment. What could be more biblical than a seeking teen, desiring God's truth, approaching a sincere parent who can give a thoughtful, sensitive, unashamed explanation of information that they need to help them resist youthful lusts? Why would this be strange or awkward? It shouldn't be. This is biblical parenting in its very essence. This should be completely normal. Somewhere along the way the typical American family strayed way off course in this area. This open communication is a very wonderful and sacred thing. It's a great honor and privilege to be able to instruct your children in such a wonderful marital gift from God. And in that context, there is no shame and no need for embarrassment.

For us, this was a tough can of worms to open at first, but our long-term goal was to establish a comfort level with our teens that would allow them to bring all of their questions, all of their struggles, and all of their temptations right to us as parents. It was a bit awkward, but over time, it became precious and very natural. I encourage you to pursue this to that point.

It is my experience with my own family and (through counseling) with many others over the years, that teens appreciate a mature and biblical approach to this subject. It gives them an alternative to hang their hopes and heart on—other than the smut and shame of the world. It shows them a remarkable and wonderful contrast between godly sex and shameful sex. It gives them a target—a hope—to look forward to the righteous, God-blessed fulfillment of physical desires within a biblical marriage.

Choose the Right Time and Age

The number one question I'm asked by parents about this matter is, *"When do I need to talk to my kids?"*

The simple answer is: *Before any one else does!*

If you have teens, we're probably already too late on that one, so there's no time to waste. There's not a magical age when all kids are "ready for this talk." There are too many variables. If your child has been abused, exposed to misinformation, or had his or her curiosity awakened—the time is *now*, regardless of their age.

If, by God's grace, you have somehow managed to protect them from being prematurely informed, then I would suggest you have your first talk in the late elementary years. It is essential that you speak of these matters before their friends do and before physical changes of adolescence begin. This is especially true for a daughter.

This is not a one-time event, but rather a gradually unfolding process. Throughout childhood and teen years, our kids should be comfortable hearing from us about these subjects and bringing their questions to us over and over again.

Get to your kids before Hollywood does, and get to your kids before their peers do. If you have failed at this, as I did with one of our children, act quickly. God will help you recover the situation, but there's no time to lose.

A Series of Conversations

The goal here is the gradual unfolding of a series of conversations that you should have with your children in progression. Hopefully those conversations will open further conversations and questions which they initiate. This is healthy. If your kids feel comfortable talking to you about sex, you have won 99% of the battle. Work at it, pray toward it, and pursue it until they do.

In short, there are three basic phases in which to have key conversations:

Phase #1, The Protection Phase—The Elementary years

One author said it this way: "Your seven-year-old son may not be thinking about sex, but I guarantee you one of his friends is!" The goal of this time is protection. Tell them enough about sex to protect them from wrong influences and situations. Don't seek to awaken their curiosity.

Usually at this phase, their young minds don't need a lot of detailed information—just guidance. I learned the hard way not to brush aside questions of curiosity. If, by some circumstance, your child has become aware of sex and is asking questions—don't brush them aside. Answer them as minimally as possible. If you don't give them answers, they will begin a quest to find them on their own, and what they discover will probably not be biblical or truthful.

Phase #2, The Connection Phase—Teen years

The goal of this time is to personally connect with your kids with more detailed and accurate information—to give them an open door to you and to have an open door to their hearts. You need to know what they are thinking. They need to bring their questions to you and to no one else. Make a deal that they should never talk to friends about this, but they can always talk to you.

During these years, recognize they can handle truth. Don't soften it, just say it with biblical respect for the subject. Don't brush off questions, and don't shame it up in any way. Reverence God's creative design with a sober mind. Treat this as sacred—not shameful or juvenile.

In addition, give them biblical and well-reasoned answers for issues of modesty, appropriateness, entertainment choices, friendship choices, etc. Teens don't respond well to "you can't watch that, wear that, do that, or hang with that crowd...*because I said so!*" They are fully capable of understanding the larger values of honoring God, obeying His truth, and valuing their own bodies as His children. Talk them through these boundaries by explaining the biblical principles and broader risks.

By the way, guard your entertainment. If you're watching suggestive innuendo on TV or in movies with your teens, you are sowing seeds of disrespect toward sexual purity. You won't like the harvest.

Phase #3, The Preparation Phase—Pre-marriage months

The goal of this time is to prepare your "about to be wed" young person for a happy honeymoon, realistic early marriage expectations, and a more deliberate and involved understanding of the details. You may opt to have a premarital counselor to help in this, but don't completely hand off the responsibility.

Christian young people who have stayed pure don't deserve to be sent into their honeymoon night with blinders on. There's too much about the honeymoon that becomes the foundation of the physical relationship throughout the early years of marriage. A young couple with misguided information, unmet expectations, ignorance, or fear will be in store for some real potential disappointments and possible early marital struggles in this area. If left unresolved, these issues can remain and literally cripple the marriage going forward.

One of the worst things you could do is show disrespect toward an appropriate sexual relationship or share honeymoon horror stories from your own marriage. Many men make light of this subject with their engaged friends, and many ladies share negative information with engaged ladies. This is harmful.

Have a goal to help your engaged son or daughter prepare for a wonderful early marital experience that can continue to grow over the decades of marriage. Be specific, be clear, be open and honest, be sensitive, but most of all—be *there!*

Give them Christian, Bible-centered materials to help prepare for those first marital, physical experiences, and help them have the right expectations and know how to deal with potential problems.

Choose the Right Approach

The second most frequent question parents ask on this topic is, "*What do I say? How specific do I get?*"

The simple answer: *Speak the truth in love.*

The book of Proverbs is the best example of a father teaching his son about sexual temptation. Proverbs 5:1–6 teach what kind of woman will bring him down. Verses 7–14 teach about the consequences and to avoid such women. Verses 15–23 teach of a pure marriage relationship. This is a complete package of sexual instruction from a father to a son. It also works for a daughter.

After you work through Proverbs 5, turn a page to chapter 7. This chapter tells the complete story of the process of sexual temptation and how one man wrecked his life.

To create a clear picture of a loving, biblical relationship, teach through Genesis 24—the story of Isaac and Rebekah. Emphasize how they were pure, godly, and honoring to their parents. Show how God brought them together with the right person at the right time. Or read through the Song of Solomon and share critical insights about godly, committed love and biblical romance.

To create a clear picture of a ruined life, turn to Judges 14 and teach through the out-of-control passions of Samson. Or go to the life of Solomon in 1 Kings 11 and teach how unrestrained sexual desires ruined the wisest man who ever lived.

Beyond these chapters, there are many passages and other examples that share principles of purity and marriage or the dangers of fornication and sexual sin. With the help of a concordance, look up biblical words like fornication and lust.

Teach your teen the truth, not just the biology. Teach them the purpose of the sexual relationship—procreation, intimacy, comfort, and marital pleasure. Teach them the value of one man and one woman for life.

Of course, all of this should be established upon the foundation of your own healthy marriage. If there are problems, neglect, or stress in your marriage, it may be difficult for you to transparently teach on these matters. It may be wise to seek counsel in strengthening your own relationship as you prepare for these vital discussions.

Here are a few practical principles for these conversations:

The answer should fit the question. Complex questions deserve thorough answers. Simple questions deserve simple answers.

Initiate the discussion. The chances are, your kids never will, but they will be glad you did.

Prepare your teens for the battle against sexual temptation. Encourage them to come to you when being tempted. In those times, pray together, memorize scripture, and talk through the struggle for purity.

Be relaxed and sensitive. Your teen will gauge your emotions and follow suit. If you are tense, they will be tense. If you are embarrassed, they will be embarrassed.

Create an approachable atmosphere in your home. If they can't come to you, they will go to someone. That's something to be tense about!

Take advantage of teaching moments. Look for open doors to teach your kids about a proper perspective about sexuality. When surrounded by a perverse culture, speak up and put it into context (i.e., "Isn't it sad that so many people are missing out on God's blessing of a great marriage?").

Use correct terms without being embarrassed. This is probably the most difficult part of the conversation. Be courageous, Game Master!

Give them a positive paradigm of sex within marriage. This is not shameful or embarrassing. It is wonderful, biblical, and healthy. The whole world is telling them that sex *now* is what life is all about. Let them know sex in marriage is well worth the wait.

Be appropriately affectionate with your spouse in front of your children. Show them that you are in love, and make it real. Don't fake it.

Don't be embarrassed about your own relationship. Be confident in the Lord, and assure your children that your marriage is healthy.

Be biblical, not just clinical. Covering the biology of this is really only about 25% of the needed discussion. Once the biology is covered, give the biblical foundation for it all.

Give them a truthfully negative paradigm of sex outside of marriage. Teach them of the pain and problems that result from fornication. You can be much more specific with them than a youth pastor or Sunday school teacher can be.

Choose the Right Context

These are special conversations that will forever be etched into the heart and memory of your teen. While the questions may arise at any time, the premeditated discussions should be thoughtfully planned. Here are a few ideas on creating a right context.

Make this event memorable. Perhaps with a purity ring or some special setting.

Choose a private setting where you can converse freely. Think through the details to help your child be comfortable.

Dads talk to sons, Moms (or Dad with Mom) talk to daughters. Dad needs to take the lead in talking with a daughter about the basics of sex and biblical values. There are, however, most likely some details that a daughter would prefer left to a private conversation with Mom.

Note: If you are a single parent, consider enlisting the help of a same-gender, spiritual mentor to talk to your child (e.g., Single dad, enlist the help of your pastor's wife.).

Make any place right for follow-up questions and conversations. Availability and approachability are essential in protecting your family. Realize you are fighting to protect the purity of those who do not yet realize its value in a world that is trying to destroy it.

As we close this chapter, I want to give you a bit of a jump-start. Again, the book *Just Friends* is filled with biblical material that would be pertinent to these conversations. Also, the following is a list of twenty reasons why sexual sin (fornication) is always self-destructive and displeasing to God:.

20 Reasons to Avoid Premarital Sex

"Flee fornication. Every sin that a man doeth is without the body; but he that committeth fornication sinneth against his own body" (1 Corinthians 6:18).

In all of my counseling, I never meet people who are glad that they have committed fornication. After the fact, there is *always* regret. Here's a list of why fornication is always a really bad idea:

1. *It breaks God's laws and dishonors Him.* Search a concordance for the word "fornication." We could stop here—it's all we really need to know.

2. *It presents huge physical risk.* Diseases and illness are rampant among those who engage in this lifestyle.

3. *It presents huge emotional risk.* A physical and emotional bond without a spiritual commitment is never a winning experience.

4. *It presents huge spiritual risk.* Grieving the Holy Spirit and offending a holy God means we forfeit God's best. We never win by dishonoring God.

5. *It is awkward, guilt ridden, unfulfilling, and not representative of God's original intent.* This is why we now have a culture that continually seeks fulfillment with new partners and relationships.

6. *It is disappointing at the physical, emotional, and spiritual levels.* The only physical intimacy that exceeds expectations is that founded on long-term commitment and marital growth.

7. *It creates a spiritual/emotional bond without commitment.* This only breeds resentment, bitterness, and the feeling of being used. It says something like this, "I don't love you enough to commit to you, but I love me enough to use you."

8. *It destroys trust.* The best way to have trust in a marriage is to stay pure before you get married. Learning to be committed to Christ (in purity) is the best way to learn to be committed to a spouse.

9. *It creates resentment and frustration.* It was designed to happen within a committed marriage of selfless love. Outside of that, fornication just breaks the heart and wounds the soul.

10. *It leaves you empty and searching for real love.* Physical intimacy doesn't create a loving, committed relationship; it's the fruit of one.

11. *It devalues the future intimacy of your marriage.* Intimacy is "just the two of us." Premarital relationships destroy that before it even happens.

12. *It prevents the greatest intimacy in marriage.* The purest and most fulfilling marital relationship is that which is forever untouched by previous relationships. (If you have failed morally, don't lose hope. Claim God's grace, and begin protecting your future marriage today by abstaining from further fornication. Jesus doesn't shame you, but He would say, "Go and sin no more.")

13. *It sets a person on a path of unfulfilling sexual experiences.* Fornication is a downward spiral of perpetually unfulfilling relationships.

14. *It attempts to shortcut God's plan for marriage and family.* It turns God's great gift of family and love into a cheap thrill and self-centered pleasure quest.

15. *It prevents you from having the most fulfilling sexual relationship.* While a person is sleeping around, they are NOT preparing for the wonderful lifetime relationship that God intended.

16. *It enlarges sexual desires and makes them insatiable.* Thinking with your hormones allows them to become an unruly taskmaster.

17. *It puts the flesh and hormones in control of your life.* You are more than a chemical reaction that seeks gratification. Don't allow your life to be directed by physical desires. Submit those desires

to the Holy Spirit, and let them be fulfilled in God's time and in God's way.

18. *It creates children without strong homes.* God intends this relationship to create a family with a foundation of commitment and lifetime love.

19. *It feeds the abortion industry.* Illicit relationships create unwanted children which creates "the abortion industry."

20. *It cannot be done safely, no matter what culture says.* Safe sex is one man and one woman, committed in marriage, for the rest of their lives.

For those who have never committed fornication, God has a simple message—DON'T (Ephesians 5:3). For those who have or who are, God also has a simple message—STOP (Acts 15:29).

God is the giver of the wonderful gift of marriage. He is the Creator of life, love, marriage, and sex. Obeying His plan is always right and always blessed.

And a life of wonderful, married intimacy is one more thing…

…well worth the wait!

15

THE PARTNERING PARENT
A Tale of Three Lost Boys and a Local Church

O*pening scene*—an unsaved, young family of five is running late to church on a Sunday morning. Three lost, longhaired, little boys (all younger than seven years old) sit quietly in the back seat of the car while a frustrated mom and dad debate over "why" they are late.

The scene is a microcosm of their lives—two frustrated adults, groping for truth and direction, fighting for a young marriage and children, and three boys romping through childhood, unaware of how desperately their family needs a miracle—they need Jesus.

Until recently, this family has rarely attended church, but they are looking for something—grasping for hope. And they hope that church will lead them to help.

Scene two—moments later, out of exasperation, dad whips the car into the driveway of the closest church, which happened to be an immediate left—"Fine then, we'll just go *here*," he spouts. *Here* could have been anywhere—but for the Divine providence of God.

Here happened to be a healthy, local, independent Baptist church—a Bible-believing church.

And while Mom and Dad are still fussing with each other, the three boys bound into the lobby and down the center aisle to find a seat close to the front. They are tired of sitting in the back of churches they have recently visited.

Congregational singing is in progress, and as Mom and Dad arrive at the door, they are immediately appalled to see that their boys have *gone rogue,* and now they must follow to the front to retrieve them. A discerning Christian quickly vacates her second-row seat for the visiting family, and seconds later all five are aligned and alert "in spitting distance" of the pulpit. Mom and Dad are embarrassed, but the boys are just glad to have a good view.

Scene three—a strong biblical message has been preached by a Spirit-filled preacher. God's Word has spoken—loudly and clearly, and His Spirit is working powerfully in the hearts of two parents on the second row.

Moments later, heads are bowed and eyes are closed. An invitation song is being sung. Three lost, little, longhaired boys stand quietly, wide-eyed, and alone on the second row. Dad and Mom have tearfully stepped out to speak with the pastor. They are taken to a room with a counselor where Dad recommits his life to Jesus, and Mom accepts Him as her personal Saviour.

The three boys are waiting with an elderly lady on the second row who graciously gives them candy and tells them, "Mommy and Daddy will be done in a moment." But the boys are in no hurry, because after all, they are eating *candy*. They now *love* this church and this lady! They are committed for life.

Fast forward five days—The young family has now attended six nights of church in a row—due to the fact that Sunday morning began a revival meeting, and the boys wanted to return every night to hear the children's stories. It is now Friday night. The oldest boy has trusted Christ as his Saviour. The two younger will soon follow. And every night of the week, this searching young family has been welcomed, loved, and nurtured in something foreign to their home—*the love of Jesus Christ in a local church filled with gracious, godly, joyful people.*

Scene four—six months have passed. Life for this young family has changed dramatically—radically—by the powerful grace of God. Attending three services each week, all five are growing in the Word, developing strong relationships, and being discipled by a patient pastor and compassionate church family. The three little boys now have a home that is being built upon Christ and a daddy and mommy who are discovering biblical principles of marriage and family that they would never have learned in any other institution.

Scene five—a year has passed. Dad and Mom have been enlisted as youth workers. A loving youth pastor has led them through a training course. They have adopted new standards of living that they might be a godly example to the youth of the church.

The training provided more than equipped youth workers. It provided a biblical framework of family and child rearing that Dad and Mom adopted at home as well. The principles proved effective with their own three sons. In short order, Dad is selected to teach the senior high teen class. As a result, he becomes an avid Bible student. What he learns, he lives. What he lives, he begins to pass on to three sets of eyes watching ever so carefully.

Pause button, please—Hold the still frame in your mind. The story continues, but we will stop here for it is much too long. The little boys all grow up to love and serve God. Daddy and Mommy stay together and become happy Grandpa and Grammy to fifteen third-generation Christians. It's a wonderful story, really. But before we walk away, we must consider—*what principles are at play in this plot?*

How did God take a rogue family and redeem them?

How did His grace radically transform and reconcile these lives? What methods and resources did He use to produce such a wonderful and miraculous story of grace and glory? How did two young Christian parents lead their three longhaired boys to love and live for God well into their adult lives?

There are three powerful biblical principles that apply directly to your life and family from this story:

First, Jesus loves, died for, and works through local church ministry. A faithful pastor who preaches the Word, a supportive staff who share in the work, a unified church family, growing, serving, loving, and laboring together—these elements, when functioning optimally by their biblical pattern, form a God-empowered force for astounding life-change. The pattern never fails. It works by the anointing grace of Almighty God.

He loves this entity. He blesses this formula. And miracles can still happen in the lives of daddies, mommies, and mop-headed little boys because of this wonderful institution called the local church. It is the single institution for which Jesus gave His life and through it He produces radical, grace-filled, life transformation to this very day.

Second, Jesus added an imperfect you to an imperfect church family as a part of His perfect plan. Some would argue today that the church is a failed entity—a flawed proposition. And they attempt a convincing argument. They point out ineffective churches and failed movements. They rehearse the failures of past church leaders. They share their own personal scars and wounds inflicted by fractured church families and carnal Christians.

But in every case, it was not God's model that was flawed. It was unspiritual people who were flawed. Flesh messes everything up. Carnality corrupts. God's pattern still works beautifully when Spirit-filled Christians allow it.

Every member of every local church is broken—human—frailty personified. One insightful pastor said it this way: "The church is a society of sinners who have finally realized it and banded themselves together to do something about it."

Thankfully, it is not the humans who make it work. It is the supernatural hand of Christ being expressed through the frailty of surrendered human beings—this is what makes the miracles. The model still works if we will allow the Holy Spirit to produce it through us.

Third, when you embrace your local church, everybody wins. Jesus placed you in His church for a purpose.

Perhaps you were the usher who handed the little boys their bulletin as they blew past you. Perhaps you were the singer who first drew this family's attention to Christ's love. Perhaps you were the janitor who prepared the room or the sound man who checked the microphones. Perhaps you were the preacher who prepared the message or the vigilant church member who gave up her seat. Perhaps you were the children's teacher who so captivatingly told the stories, or the elderly lady who obeyed the Holy Spirit and remembered the candy! Perhaps you were the youth leader who trained or the summer intern who demonstrated the joy of Christianity. Perhaps you were the faithful tither, the prayer warrior, or the behind-the-scenes servant.

Whoever you were in the story, you were vital. Without you, the story is interrupted, halted. Perhaps prevented altogether.

Because you serve, *everybody wins.*

You win because you get to invest your abilities and resources into something eternally valuable.

Your family wins because you all get to grow and serve God together in a loving family. Your whole family gets to develop life-long relationships in an abundantly joyful place.

Your church family wins because the work of God goes forward through your faithful service and sacrifice.

Your community wins because the love of Christ is personified—you become the heart and hands of Jesus changing your city.

And best of all—little, lost boys and their parents win because their lives are forever transformed through the amazing love of Christ. *The local church gives a kind of love that isn't found in any other place on Earth!*

Jesus Christ is still pleased to work through faithful, imperfect church families for His perfect purposes. The local church is it! It's the place. It's the plan. It's the one entity on the planet established by God where His miracles continue to unfold—one heart at a time.

I love the local church. Jesus loves the local church.

Wise parents are partnering parents. They partner with a local church. They lock arms with a Bible-believing, Bible-preaching pastor and gracious church family. They embrace a commitment to attending, giving, serving, and growing with their pastor and church family. They find a godly man and follow his biblical faith as he follows Christ.

"Remember them which have the rule over you, who have spoken unto you the word of God: whose faith follow, considering the end of their conversation" (Hebrews 13:7).

Turn your heart toward Christ by finding the local church where He desires to implant you and your family. Immerse your heart wholly into that church. Invest into that church. Love and encourage others in that church. Support and pray for the pastor and staff of that church. Get involved in serving in that church. Put your abilities, gifts, and resources to work in that which God says He loves—in that which Christ purchased on the cross.

You will not find a better investment of your life, your time, your energy, your money, your talents, or your resources. You will never, in a million years, if you searched the entire galaxy, find a better team with which to partner in bringing up your family in the ways of Christ.

This is the pinnacle of perfect investment and growth opportunities—an investment into that which changes hearts. It will change yours and your kids' hearts. And together, God will use you to change others.

How do I know? Why do I so confidently assert that the local church is God's plan for bringing searching hearts to Christ? How can I so passionately believe in the miracle of life-change through the local church? Why do I know that wise parents are partnering parents? Because I was there.

The miracle happened to me. I was the oldest of the three long-haired little boys—who are no longer lost.

"Husbands, love your wives, even as Christ also loved the church, and gave himself for it; That he might sanctify and cleanse it with the washing of water by the word, That he might present it to himself a glorious church, not having spot, or wrinkle, or any such thing; but that it should be holy and without blemish" (Ephesians 5:25–27).

"So we, being many, are one body in Christ, and every one members one of another" (Romans 12:5).

"To the intent that now unto the principalities and powers in heavenly places might be known by the church the manifold wisdom of God, According to the eternal purpose which he purposed in Christ Jesus our Lord" (Ephesians 3:10–11).

"Unto him be glory in the church by Christ Jesus throughout all ages, world without end. Amen" (Ephesians 3:21).

"…That ye stand fast in one spirit, with one mind striving together for the faith of the gospel" (Philippians 1:27).

Practical Thoughts for the Partnering Parent

Commit to a Bible-preaching local church. The New Testament provides a very clear picture of what Jesus intends His church to be. In today's culture there are, among Bible-believing churches, two unbiblical extremes.

The first is the worldly church. In many forms and on many levels, this church is simply conforming to and in love with the world. In 1 John 2:15 we are commanded to *"love not the world."* Ephesians 5:11 teaches that we are to separate from the *"unfruitful works of darkness, but rather reprove them."* You are wise to avoid a church that weakens doctrine and welcomes carnality. It's difficult to *"be not conformed to this world, but be ye transformed"* (Romans 12:2) if your church home is immersed in worldliness.

The second is the segregated church. In an effort to avoid worldly and failed church models, many are retreating into home worship or "home churches" that have only minor resemblances to the functioning and mission-oriented local churches of the New Testament. Somewhat out of fear, some parents are choosing to segregate themselves from even healthy local church congregations. This is not consistent with the New Testament pattern of local church ministry.

A biblical local church (like those profiled early in the chapter) wins the lost with the Gospel, disciples new believers to maturity, and strives together for the faith of the Gospel (Philippians 1:27). There is no perfect church, but there are plenty of healthy ones.

Follow a godly pastor and spiritual influences. Spiritual leadership is a part of God's plan for every Christian home. Ephesians 4:11 calls these spiritual leaders gifts from God. Hebrews 13 admonishes us to remember them, acknowledge them, and follow their faith. Wise parents partner with humble, godly, transparent spiritual leaders—pastors, assistant pastors, teachers, coaches, etc.—who will serve and encourage the spiritual growth of the whole family.

One of the most unwise things you can do is have "roast Pastor and roast church" for lunch every Sunday. Parents who criticize spiritual authorities merely undermine their own spiritual foundation and that of their children. These kids grow up and usually leave church because they simply have no respect for the church or its leaders.

Serve together with a ministry-focused family. This is one of the best secrets of church life! Parents and teens can serve God together. Get into a ministry and do something together for others and for the Gospel.

Ask God to let you lead someone to Jesus with your child. And when He does, go celebrate together afterwards. The greatest family memories can and should be those of growing up in a healthy local church, serving together, striving together with other joyful believers.

"Only let your conversation be as it becometh the gospel of Christ: that whether I come and see you, or else be absent, I may hear of your affairs, that ye stand fast in one spirit, with one mind striving together for the faith of the gospel" (Philippians 1:27).

Have a family mission or calling. What is your family working towards? Why do you exist as a team? Is your family life merely a humdrum experience of monotonous and repetitive routines with no bigger picture playing out? It shouldn't be. Both you and your kids should be absolutely captivated by a larger mission—a Jesus-centered, Gospel-centered purpose. You should all be on God's mission, together with your church family, helping to fulfill His ultimate, eternal redemptive plan.

Have a generous and hospitable home. Shortly after my parents came to Christ, I witnessed a marvelous, grace-generated transformation in their lives. My Mom and Dad became dynamic Christians with generous and hospitable hearts. There was hardly a week that my Mom wasn't cleaning the house and making tacos as we hosted other Christians and spiritual influences into our living room.

There wasn't anyone Mom wasn't willing to serve or encourage. Over and over she gave herself and her home away to others. Dad and Mom became youth workers, and Dad taught the senior high. Our lives were continually abuzz with teen groups, Bible college interns, guest evangelists, Sunday evening fellowships, and Christian friends.

In addition to this, I watched my parents tithe, give generously, and bless others as a result of God's blessings in our lives. Thirty-five years later, people still tell me on a regular basis, "Your parents were an amazing blessing to us!" Their legacy lives on.

To a ten-year-old boy, all that time with all those abundantly joyful servants of God was incredibly inspiring. Why wouldn't I want to love and serve Jesus?! These people were the loudest laughing, happiest people I had ever seen. In my estimation, I was incredibly blessed to have gracious, giving parents and so many wonderful, godly influences.

Local church partnerships are God-ordained. In spite of the broken state of many churches and the disparity between Bible Christianity and the way some Christians live, God's people and great local churches are still His primary tool for genuine life transformation!

Decide today that you will be a Christian committed to local church life—as Jesus desires. Decide that you will be a partnering parent—and grandparent!

16

THE SHEPHERDING PARENT

Seeing the Danger and Leading the Right Direction

God's Word says in Job 6:30, *"Is there iniquity in my tongue? cannot my taste discern perverse things?"* In this passage, Job is defending the purity of his heart, and he references *discernment* in the form of a word picture. He compares his ability to discern good and evil in his own heart to his ability to taste good and perverse things with his tongue.

As parents, our spiritual discernment should be as acute as our physical taste. Our spiritual taste buds should be sensitive to discern good and evil, but this isn't the case in today's culture. In fact, for many Christian parents, our spiritual taste buds are all but dead. We've allowed the world's philosophy to cloud our thinking, numb our hearts, and deaden our sensitivity to spiritual things.

The prophet Ezekiel wrote in Ezekiel 44:23, *"And they shall teach my people the difference between the holy and profane, and cause them to discern between the unclean and the clean."* God desires that we learn discernment. He wants us to have sensitive taste buds to that which is clean versus that which is unclean. And He wants us to teach our children the same.

One of the most detrimental developments in Christian families in recent years is a deadening of spiritual discernment. We have lost some of our perception of what is clean and unclean—holy and profane. We have become tolerant and even accepting of sin. We have lowered our standards and deadened our hearts to that which displeases the Lord.

It's time that we awaken our taste buds. It's time that we regain a God-given sensitivity to right and wrong in our homes. If we are going to raise godly children, we must be able to discern the arsenal of our enemy.

God commands us to *"walk circumspectly, not as fools, but as wise"* (Ephesians 5:15). He commands us to walk through life diligently looking in all directions—wary of our enemy and alert to his relentless attempts to penetrate our homes. Ask God daily to enlighten the eyes of your understanding and to help you see what others cannot.

"The eyes of your understanding being enlightened; that ye may know what is the hope of his calling, and what the riches of the glory of his inheritance in the saints" (Ephesians 1:18).

Discernment is a product of the Word of God and the wisdom of God. You must daily hear, study, and apply God's Word to your parenting, and you must daily ask God to give you wisdom.

Discernment will ultimately require action—courage. When you discern something harmful, it will take courage to step into the gap and take action. Your teenager may not understand why he cannot watch that show, listen to that song, hang around that friend, or visit that website. She may even fight you on it.

Go with your "gut," spiritually speaking. Don't ignore the prompting and leading of the Holy Spirit in your heart when He is trying to give you discernment. Don't second-guess Him. Just explain to your teenager that you are discerning something harmful. Your young person will ultimately appreciate your committed love.

As we ask the Lord for discernment, I believe there are three primary "kinds" of hidden dangers that catch families by surprise.

Satanic Dangers

The first hidden danger is what I would call "satanic danger." These things don't always appear to be directly "satanic" on the surface, but clearly, they have a direct link to satanic or demonic influences.

Ephesians 6:12 teaches us clearly *"For we wrestle not against flesh and blood, but against principalities, against powers, against the rulers of the darkness of this world, against spiritual wickedness in high places."* Again in 2 Corinthians 10:4, Paul wrote, *"(For the weapons of our warfare are not carnal, but mighty through God to the pulling down of strong holds;)."*

Lest you think I'm merely being sensational or spooky—take God at His Word. Accept the truth that there is a dark, spiritual enemy fighting hard for the heart of your teenager. Our goal as parents must be to stand guard over young hearts—to recognize that we fight an invisible foe who is aggressive and cunning. This battle is spiritual. We must open our eyes and see our true enemy for who he is—for only then can we resist his attacks.

While it seems the devil's tricks are innumerable, there are a few that stand out blatantly to me in my ongoing work with families. What are these "satanic dangers?" Let's examine a few.

Dark role playing games—Many of these types of games are purely satanic in their origin, but they are cleverly disguised. Without a doubt they open the heart to spiritual oppressive influences, and they become strongholds in young lives.

Dark or violent online or video games—These games are breeding grounds for anger, rebellion, and enormous future problems. Be aware of every game your child plays and make sure it isn't connected with dark kinds of violence. I'd say you're pretty safe with football, basketball, and PGA golf. Suffice to say, we've come a long way since "Super Mario Brothers" and "Ms. PacMan."

Dark music—While there are many forms of harmful music, this kind is blatantly and unapologetically satanic in nature. The performers, writers, and producers openly admit this.

Fascination with wicked men or events—Why do kids idolize Hitler, draw satanic symbols on their notebooks, and relish horrific historic events? Something very dark, demonic, and dangerous is happening in the heart of a young person caught up in these things.

Association with dark-minded friends—Many parents don't feel that they have the right to control their child's friendships, yet if your teen is gravitating to the wrong crowd, you must commit to rebuilding your own relationship with him or her. Kids usually choose a bad crowd because their relationships at home are nearly non-existent. The common neglect or common misery brings struggling kids together.

Fascination with dark or violent entertainment—Demonic and cultic movies, dark TV shows, and horror novels are nothing to play with. These things all have a strong and satanic effect on the heart.

Media about witchcraft, demonism, or sorcery—Witchcraft and sorcery are dangerous in any form, no matter how entertaining or playful.

Fixation with wearing black—This is more of an indicator than a cause, but it is enough to cause concern. I'm not saying there's something sinful about wearing black. I'm saying that satanic involvement in young lives often manifests itself with a fixation for only black.

Years ago I did a funeral for a young teen killed in an automobile accident. At the graveside I spent an hour talking with one of her Satanist friends who confirmed with me that teens who consistently dress in black are almost always involved in the occult. These warnings may sound like paranoia or extremism, but check out recent headlines of school shootings and you may feel differently.

Obsessive, Compulsive Dangers

There are many behaviors in our technologically advanced culture that could not be considered sinful or wicked on the surface, but by their very nature can become obsessive and compulsive—or addictive.

Before we find out what they are, consider two important facts. First, some of these things in moderation are innocent, and some are even helpful. Second, teens don't live in a world of "moderation." Not only do they not know what the word means, they tend to struggle with doing things "moderately." They lean toward youthful obsession. Whether it's a song, a boyfriend or girlfriend, a TV show, a skateboard, a video game, or a clothing style—they gravitate to extremes. Teens are intensely faddish and fickle. While they are supposed to grow out of it, frankly some don't, and it is our responsibility as parents to teach them to live soberly and with biblical moderation.

"Let your moderation be known unto all men. The Lord is at hand" (Philippians 4:5).

"That the aged men be sober, grave, temperate, sound in faith, in charity, in patience. The aged women likewise, that they be in behaviour as becometh holiness, not false accusers, not given to much wine, teachers of good things;

That they may teach the young women to be sober, to love their husbands, to love their children, To be discreet, chaste, keepers at home, good, obedient to their own husbands, that the word of God be not blasphemed. Young men likewise exhort to be sober minded. In all things shewing thyself a pattern of good works: in doctrine shewing uncorruptness, gravity, sincerity, Sound speech, that cannot be condemned; that he that is of the contrary part may be ashamed, having no evil thing to say of you" (Titus 2:2–8).

Almost anything can become an idol, but, in an effort to keep the list short, here are just a few things that are currently dominating today's youth culture in a negative way.

Internet surfing/gaming—A short study of technology will reveal that the more time we connect with the Internet, the less time we connect with each other. Beware of the way that Satan tries to replace real family relationships with "cyber-life."

Social networking—Much social networking is either blatantly perverse or gossip and contention oriented. There are exceptions, and there should be. Don't allow Facebook to become an addiction for you or your teen.

Text messaging—Yes, text messaging can be immensely useful and helpful. But many young people allow it to become an obsessive, compulsive addiction. This is a rather innocent tool that easily becomes an unhealthy obsession.

Video gaming—In our culture, video games have become a replacement for home relationships, and this is greatly limiting our children's potential. Fun is fine in moderation, but guard the time, the music, the content, and the extremes in this area.

Skate boarding/extreme sports—I'm not opposed to having a great time in some energetic sport or hobby, but the sad part of the extreme sports culture is that it's not merely about fun—it's about a cult-like lifestyle, rock music, and living wildly. There may be nothing wrong with a snowboard or motorcycle or a board with wheels attached to it. Enjoy these things with your kids if you can, but teach them and guard them from the accompanying companions, culture, and sinful lifestyle.

Dating/obsessive friendships—During the teen years, obsession with boys or girls can become a growth-halting factor. Parents must be vigilant to shepherd through these new emotions. In addition to this, young people often pick one friend and latch on to that friend obsessively. These kinds of dominant friendships can take priority over the Lord, over family, and over important life values.

At times these things could fit the Bible word *folly*, which means silliness at a simple level or at a morally perverse level. Folly is whatever diverts your teenager away from growing in godliness.

Passive Behavioral Dangers

Passive behavioral dangers are more or less warning signs of something wrong in the heart—red flags if you will. They deserve our parental insight and attention.

These warning signs do not involve what the young person is actively *doing* as much as what he is *not* doing—what he or she is avoiding. Often we miss these dangers because we're asking the wrong questions.

Rather than merely asking "what's wrong with it?" we should be asking "what's right with it?" or "is this as right as it could be?"

In James 4:17 the Bible says, *"Therefore to him that knoweth to do good, and doeth it not, to him it is sin."* Often the proof of a wrong spiritual direction is seen in "what they are avoiding" or what they are choosing not to do. There are many times that a teenager deliberately avoids right without actually engaging blatantly in wrong. If our parenting philosophy is based upon a "they're not doing anything wrong" mentality, we will miss these important red flags.

Here are a few of the more prominent passive warning signs.

Dressing disrespectfully for respectful environments—For many kids, this is just a matter of training—not a problem of the heart. Yet, often dress is a statement of rebellion or disrespect that calls for some parental leadership and training.

Avoiding participation in spiritual environments—Some Christians automatically gravitate toward the farthest possible position from the Word of God and from well-lit, open areas. Shy? Maybe. We could reason that there's nothing *wrong* with this, but it certainly could be an indicator of a disengaged heart.

Disrespectful posture—Some kids suddenly have serious posture issues any time the Bible or an authority figure arrives on the scene. They sit normally at other times, but they assume a physical posture of resistance to God. Perhaps it's a maturity/training issue, perhaps it's a statement—discernment will seek to understand.

Choosing carnal friends—As a parent you have the responsibility to guide and direct your child's choices of friends, but there's a deeper issue. Gravitating toward struggling friends is a big red flag of a struggling heart. More than merely trying to control the friend choices (the fruit issue) we must deal with the root issue of a right heart with God and a close relationship parentally. A heart that sincerely seeks to please God will naturally connect with similar hearts.

Retreating in isolation—Teenagers like to hang out with friends. But those with pure hearts and clear consciences don't mind being around adults either. When your child immediately darts for the darkest or most isolated area to sequester with friends, it's usually because there's something to hide.

Avoiding spiritual influences—Satan attacks healthy relationships. A sincere teenager will always appreciate and respond healthily to good influences who are doing their best to teach them and direct them toward Jesus. When a wedge is driven between these relationships (and that happens as we will see in chapter 18), you are wise to lead your child to resolve those concerns in person with those influences.

Secluding to their rooms for extended periods of time—While there's nothing wrong with solace, teens ought to desire to spend time with their family. They should sometimes be asking you, "Hey, what are we going to do tonight as a family?" Give focused time and prayer to rebuilding the relationship that's been lost if your teen has developed the habit of constant isolation and seclusion. (Homework or personal devotions are the obvious exceptions.)

Teens Need Pastoring More than Pushing

One final thought. Don't panic and freak out if you read this chapter and see these "warning signs" in the life of your teen. Your gut reaction might be to overreact and start pushing your teen towards a safer and more spiritual position. This will come across as too little, too late, and will look more like a desperate grasp for control rather than a genuine response of concern and leadership.

God speaks of pastoring in Jeremiah. Look at these two verses:

"And I will give you pastors according to mine heart, which shall feed you with knowledge and understanding" (Jeremiah 3:15).

"For the pastors are become brutish, and have not sought the LORD: *therefore they shall not prosper, and all their flocks shall be scattered"* (Jeremiah 10:21).

In the first verse, God desired for His people to be pastored (literally pastured, tended, fed) with knowledge and understanding. This, again, is nurture and instruction. It is loving leadership.

In the second verse, God was indicting the pastors who were "brutish" and acting without God's leadership. The word *brutish* means to consume, to burn in anger, to eat up. This is the natural response of many parents.

Think of it this way: *you can push them, or you can lead them.* Teens always respond better to leadership than they do to "pusher-ship." (I know, that's not a word—it's literary license. But it works.)

Don't be a brutish parent—burning in wrath towards children who really belong to the Lord. Be a shepherding parent—gently and courageously leading in the paths of righteousness and away from sin. Feed them with knowledge and understanding.

Right now, take a moment to ask God for discernment. Then ask Him to help you become the shepherding parent that He desires for you to be.

17

THE TECHNO-SAVVY PARENT
Whacking the Media Monster

One night a few years ago, my wife and I decided to stay up late to work on some projects. I chose to stay in my chair in the living room, while she chose to sit up in bed and work—both of us on our laptops. Before long, we were both thinking of things we needed to tell each other, and so we began to send off little emails to each other.

I'm embarrassed to admit this, but after about thirty minutes it occurred to both of us that we were only about 40 feet apart! My wife wrote me and said, "Why are we doing this?" That's when it hit me— we're so connected in this culture that we don't even have to talk to each other anymore.

We've never been more "connected"—or less connected. The average home in America has multiple devices for every member of the family. We're the most technologically advanced culture on the planet, but we're paying a devastating price for it in our homes.

Admittedly, I'm a huge gadget-junkie myself, but before we get too carried away (or has that already happened?), let's pause for a moment.

Connected but Disconnected

Much of the message of this book is about *regaining* and *retaining* your connection as a family. And one of the greatest threats to that connection is the media in our homes. In many cases, we've wired our kids directly to the world so we can work more, make more, and live more apart from them. Family life is not supposed to be this way.

It's time to reconnect! Our kids shouldn't be on Facebook more than they are with you—talking, relating, laughing, enjoying, playing, praying, being loved, accepted, nurtured, and trained up. They belong close to your heart, and you belong close to theirs.

Beware of the Creep-Factor

I have a deep inner aversion to living things that crawl, creep, fly, or slither around and find their way into places they don't belong. They bother me. They creep me out. I just want them dead as quickly as I can make it happen. It's not really fear (or so I want you to believe)—it's more about my human right to "not be creeped out!" (After all, it's in everybody's basic rights—life, liberty, the pursuit of happiness, and the freedom to be uncreeped.)

Not long ago, I had a bat in my office. Another time, a bird came flying in—yes, a *bird*—into my third-floor office! Shortly thereafter, a lizard showed up in a secretary's office. And as you might imagine, these things not only hindered workflow, they significantly raised the threat level on the "creep-o-meter" in the surrounding offices. They were nasty little living things that found their way into areas they didn't belong. They disturbed and disrupted, and they had to be dealt with. And in each case—they were. The sentence was "death by broomstick."

In much the same way, only on a spiritual level, media is constantly and forever trying to creep its way into places it doesn't belong—in our hearts and homes. The message of that media depends upon our day-to-day choices—who we communicate with, what we listen to, what we post, what we watch or play, and who we follow or befriend. These tools and resources are not all bad. In many ways they can and should be used for good—but unrestrained and unmoderated they present some serious risks.

Simply put: media will eat your family alive unless you tell it not to.

Sacrificing the Next Generation

The most tragic result of our disconnected tendencies is that we are losing our kids (from Christian homes) at an alarming rate. As our Christian teens are graduating from high school, we're seeing a large percentage of them toss God in the back seat (or out the back window) and launch out into a "have it my way" future of self-centered living.

To the southwest of Jerusalem is a deep ravine with steep, rocky cliffs called the Valley of Hinnom. In Old Testament times, it was a horrible place of idolatry and pagan worship. In God's Word it was where the children of Israel committed *abominations* and *evil works*. Namely— they sacrificed their infants in burnt offerings to the pagan god Molech. Notice in these few verses how God warns them of this horrific sin and how they rebelled at His Word:

"*And thou shalt not let any of thy seed pass through the fire to Molech, neither shalt thou profane the name of thy God: I am the* LORD" (Leviticus 18:21).

"*There shall not be found among you any one that maketh his son or his daughter to pass through the fire, or that useth divination, or an observer of times, or an enchanter, or a witch*" (Deuteronomy 18:10).

"*But he walked in the way of the kings of Israel, yea, and made his son to pass through the fire, according to the abominations of the heathen, whom the* LORD *cast out from before the children of Israel*" (2 Kings 16:3).

"*And they caused their sons and their daughters to pass through the fire, and used divination and enchantments, and sold themselves to do evil in the sight of the* LORD, *to provoke him to anger*" (2 Kings 17:17).

We may not struggle today with the horrific concept of sacrificing a child on a literal pagan altar. Yet, we often sacrifice them on other altars—which are no less pagan. These are altars of culture, technology, work, entertainment, materialism, ministry, and overtime. (Yes, the idea of sacrificing your family on the altar of even *ministry* is pagan.)

If you are courageous and serious enough to confront this cultural current that is rapidly pulling families apart, be prepared for resistance. Your clients, your culture, and even your kids will probably at first resist the priority shift. Yet, the struggle is worth it.

You may turn down overtime, put a new career on hold, see your financial picture grow more slowly, say goodbye to a needed promotion, or give up your favorite TV show or hobby—but these are small prices to pay to recover the heart of your child and to set his or her feet upon the solid rock of Christ.

The Solution—Segregation or Preparation?

I recognize that we live in a media-driven culture, and in many ways we are dependent upon these devices for the flow of communication and information. For this reason, I don't believe that "self-segregation" is the right response. Simply removing yourself and your children from all media is not the *nurturing* response. At some point, your child will enter adulthood—either prepared or unprepared to deal with the Internet, cell phones, computers, etc.

These things are not going away, and your child will be forced to face them at some time or another. The only biblical parenting solution is *preparation*. It's our responsibility to *prepare* and *instruct* our children to choose right.

Several years ago the LA Times reported on a Kaiser Family Foundation study that showed kids are now averaging fifty-three hours per week engaged in some form of digital media—including TV, video games, cell phones, computers, etc. This does not include when kids are multitasking—perhaps using their phone and watching TV at the same time. When factoring those numbers, the usage jumps to about seventy-five hours per week—an astounding number.

The most interesting fact presented was the impact of parental oversight. When parents engage, set boundaries, and train their children, those same kids averaged three hours less per day—twenty-one hours less in a week. That's a pretty powerful difference.

God's Word teaches us in Proverbs 29:15, "*...a child left to himself bringeth his mother to shame.*" The clarion call to parents in the midst of such a media saturated society is "train the children." This goes against the grain of two extremes.

The first extreme is unrestraint. Some parents literally leave their children to themselves, turning them over to a reckless onslaught of harmful content flowing from multiple directions. (Remember Eli.) Kids left to themselves just don't know what to do with this. They are easily overcome with temptation and sin. This is the typical overly permissive approach.

The second extreme is "self-segregation." This is simply unprincipled abstinence—the decision to remove all media from our lives without explanation or biblical training. This approach results in our children eventually facing the media monster alone in their adult lives with no biblical foundation on which to stand. This is the typical overly protective approach.

In the first extreme, media becomes dominant in the home and relationships die early. In the second, media is simply postponed to ravage an unprepared life later.

What's the balance? *Nurture and instruction with engaged oversight.*

We must set limits, teach values, provide oversight, manage accountability, and train our children how to guard their hearts. Here's a simple guideline when it comes to managing our family media:

If you allow it, you must understand it, manage it, and train children how to honorably use it.

Are your kids spending the equivalent of a full-time job using media? If so, it falls to you to understand that media—to become a techno-savvy parent. Then, you must attentively lead and monitor the use of that media.

My Kids Know More about This than I Do

Secular sociologists and psychologists have some terms for how they describe the development of a culture or society of people over multiple generations. In general, there are three types of developmental cycles among people groups:

Pre-figurative—In a pre-figurative culture, the parents teach the children, and the children learn from the parents. The entire society is built upon this model—the previous generation training up the next one.

Co-figurative—In a co-figurative culture, the children and parents share equal co-dependence. They both learn from the other. Neither one really has the upper hand of how to function well in this society. Both are simultaneously figuring it out together. This is prevalent in societies where rapid change is unfolding or where major societal upheaval has taken place—disasters, governmental coups, wars, etc.

Post-figurative—In a post-figurative culture, the parents learn from the children, and the children teach the parents. Some significant and rapid cultural shift has left the parents behind, and it falls to the children to take the lead and help the previous generation find their way. This is very common in immigrant households where the cultural language is a secondary language for the parents, but a first language for the children. The children often lead these families and teach the parents how to live and relate in their present context.

Some sociologists believe that America has come through all three developmental cycles—and is presently in the third. You can imagine the danger of this state. Obviously the biblical developmental cycle is *pre-figurative.*

There is no doubt that media and technology are the greatest factors in why our present culture, in many ways, is *post-figurative.*

If you haven't figured this out by now, you can't afford to have a post-figurative home, regardless of what the rest of our culture is doing.

If there is presently technology at use in your home—a cell phone, a satellite dish, a computer, an Xbox, etc.—that your kids know more about than you do, it can't remain that way. (However, I must admit, I still lose significantly to my sons on pretty much every Xbox game I've played.)

Parents beholden to their child's knowledge of media devices have allowed a post-figurative culture to develop in their homes. The children have become the teachers. This is unhealthy. As a first step, make a beeline for a co-figurative relationship—sit down with your teenager and learn from one another. Then, move beyond that and you become the leader of the media age in your home.

If your family is going to survive the media deluge, you're going to have to become a techno-parent and a training parent. You must be circumspect, walking wisely, and intentional about redeeming your time and preparing your children.

Proverbs 22:6 teaches us, *"Train up a child in the way he should go: and when he is old, he will not depart from it."* The process of "training up" is a time-consuming, fully engaged, active, and deliberate course of action. Yet, few parents intentionally determine to "train up" their children in managing mass media.

Some parents desire to "train up," but they feel overwhelmed or are not sure where to begin. Yet, the risk is too great not to jump on this beast and ride it into submission. Honestly, we're all still learning, and media is ever-changing. About the time you have it figured out, software makers release another update, so buckle up for a continual learning curve.

Regardless of those changes, there are five ongoing challenges that media brings into our homes. Let's take a quick look at them and then discuss a course of action.

Five Challenges Media Presents

The challenge of perversion—The media of our culture has given a loud and long voice to massive amounts of perversion. It's difficult to even buy a gallon of milk without having to see and hear the filth of our world being broadcast or displayed. Even the conservative news outlets are shameless when it comes to advertising or stories having to do with sexual matters. This challenge threatens our purity, and God commands us to flee youthful lusts (2 Timothy 2:22) and to be wise to that which is good and simple concerning evil (Romans 16:19).

The challenge of deception—The media industry is constantly heralding Satan's lies about love, happiness, and life. Additionally, the Internet gives someone a lot of opportunities to "be someone else" or to participate in gossip, slander, and harmful discourse. The myth of anonymity has drawn many into second lives, inappropriate relationships, and deceptive communications. But God tells us in James 4:8 to cleanse our hands, purify our hearts from double-mindedness, and draw nigh to God once again.

"Draw nigh to God, and he will draw nigh to you. Cleanse your hands, ye sinners; and purify your hearts, ye double minded" (James 4:8).

The challenge of obsession—Email, Twitter, Facebook, blogs, cell phones, video games, Internet forums, and a variety of other media tend to become dominant in our lives. Frankly, these mediums impact us in ways we don't even fully understand yet. Science has only just begun to examine the power that these things can have over us and the developmental results over time.

Practically speaking, in counseling, I've seen that these things can literally become obsessions—almost holding us hostage and causing us to disengage from real relationships. But in 1 Corinthians 6:12 God instructs us not to be *"brought under the power of any"*—speaking of things that may not be evil, but also may not be expedient (or helpful).

The challenge of disconnection—Media is so dominant in some families that it has completely overrun real family connections. Abundance of media kills time, robs focus, shortens attention span, and makes human relationships seem boring and shallow. But Ephesians 4:32 and 6:1–4 teach us to develop loving, tenderhearted, nurturing relationships in our homes.

The challenge of emptiness—This is the result of the first four challenges. When media is allowed to "take over," everyone in the family is familiar with everything in the world except each other, and that leaves the heart very empty and hungry. Solomon said in Ecclesiastes 1:17 that he gave his heart to know madness and folly, and ultimately it was nothing but *"vexation of spirit."*

Action Items for Vigilant Parents

Tenaciously purify your home. The enemy often gets to our kids through the back door of things we're selfishly holding onto as parents. Are you willing to give up what might be harmful to your teenager? Many parents are not. Music, movies, Internet, and a host of other things need to be well-moderated and monitored in our homes to protect our hearts.

Get on a media learning curve. Just like driving a car—first you learn, then you teach. The principle is the same with media. Refuse to have media outlets or gadgets in your home that you do not understand.

Train your children in the proper use of each media tool you allow. Again, like driving, you wouldn't toss your sixteen-year-old the keys and say, "Go figure it out." A learner's permit requires that you ride along first, showing the way and correcting the mistakes. While this is annoying to the teen and harrowing to the parent, staying alive makes it ultimately "worth it." Take the same approach to media. Get in the experience and teach and train along the way—correcting, instructing, and nurturing with biblical wisdom.

Set ground rules, protected entry points, and checkpoints. Teach your child the rules of the road, install filtering software, and grab that cell phone and iPod periodically just to monitor how it's being used. This is essential, and there is a wide variety of services (some for free) that help parents monitor their children as they use tools like email, instant messaging, online activity, text messaging, etc. In addition to this, take advantage of helpful resources like review sites that inform parents of the content of movies, TV shows, etc. Get informed and stay informed.

Be familiar with every form of media in your child's life. Trust nothing when it comes to media. Know what music they listen to, what books they read, what shows they watch, what people they follow, and what they post. Make no apology—for you cannot train up a child unless you are immersed in this world with them.

Provide clear and biblical boundaries and limitations. You may opt completely out of one form of media or another. You may restrict emails to a short list of people you know. You may limit access to only a few websites. You may determine to allow certain things at specific ages. You will definitely need to set time limits. Remember, "what someone else's parents allow" is completely irrelevant. You must set boundaries that God leads you to set. This book can't answer all of the possible scenarios, but the Holy Spirit can guide you as you ask God for wisdom.

Provide healthy alternatives to media. Help your kids stay in balance by practicing moderation (Philippians 4:5). Lead your children to read, play games, learn an instrument, play a sport, develop a hobby, or find interests that don't involve screensavers and status updates.

At times, just unplug on purpose. Have times when media is just put away, turned off, unplugged, or even taken away for a time. For instance, have a week without TV or a month with no video games.

If you really want to get a feel for how powerful your child's cell phone is, ask to look at it for a moment and read the text messages that come in. If this creates World War III, then "Houston, we have a problem." If your children can survive without these things and if they don't mind you looking at their world of communications and content, that's a good sign that they are learning appropriateness and moderation. If they freak out, that's a good sign you need to be more involved in the "train up" stuff.

The Power of OFF

Start now—today. Tonight. Do something extreme! Do something that will make your family look "freakish" in today's society. Use the OFF buttons. Take a walk. Read a book. Have a conversation. Play a game. Laugh a little. Pray as a family. Be intentionally together and intentionally simple concerning the evils of our media-crazed culture. Be old-fashioned—family—fun!

A high-connection family is a lot more important than a high-speed connection. Be a high-connection parent. Keep your heart plugged in to your kids and keep theirs plugged in to you. Keep God first and foremost in your family life and defy the odds.

Decide that yours will be a well-connected home—every heart connected to the other with high-speed access. You'll discover something—you probably forgot how much you really love (and like) these people you live with.

Parent, it is *possible* to tame the media tools of our lives. Better yet, it is possible to use them for good and for God. I hope you desire to train up the next generation to use media in a way that pleases the Lord and advances His kingdom. Don't let the media monster rampage through your home. Bring it into containment—tell it where to be, what to be, and how to be—and don't ever back down.

Remember, if you allow it, you must understand it.

Media will eat your family alive unless you tell it not to.

Part Four

DISCIPLINED
LIVES

18

THE PEACEABLE PARENT
Leading Our Children from Social Stress to Spiritual Maturity

"How'd your day go, buddy?" I was crouching down by Larry's bed to pray with him before he went to sleep. He was in fourth grade, and I'll never forget his response.

"I lost all of my friends today." He spoke in his typical low, flat tone with very little emotion. It broke my heart.

"How could you have possibly lost all your friends in one day?" I was in doubt.

"I don't know. They just all said they don't like me any more."

Now, I can't fully recall what happened that day, but I know a few things.

First, whatever traumatic social events unfolded that day left Larry feeling friendless.

Second, no parent ever wants a child to feel that way.

Third, he was probably as much at fault as all of his ex-friends.

Fourth, somewhere between fourth grade and his senior year of high school, he and his friends worked it all out.

Fifth, he didn't need me or Mom to "freak-out" about it.

And finally, God allowed him to go through that situation to grow and to develop his youthful relational skills.

Had we overreacted, become defensive, called the principal, and gotten angry at all the other kids and parents, we would have done nothing but made a mess and helped Larry miss a vital growing moment. He wouldn't have discovered that with or without friends, he still has Jesus, he still has Dad and Mom, and he's going to be okay. Those are valuable lessons.

What do you do when your teens have a meltdown in their relational world? It happens. It happens in every school, every church, and every youth group. It happens because all of our kids can be carnal—even mine and yours—and they need to learn how to love like Jesus loves.

Note: As a matter of context, please understand there is a level of social conflict that should be confronted and dealt with head on. If a child is being physically threatened, bullied, or in some way seriously mistreated—these things require the intervention of authority. This is not the context of this chapter. The focus here is on navigating the everyday tension of growing up with other human beings—like sibling rivalries.

A Defensive Spirit and Self-Segregation

Today, the typical parental response to social conflict or injustice is a defensive spirit and self-segregation. The thinking goes like this: "If my child is having a hard time in this environment, it's the *environment's* fault. I will remove my child and find another environment." There are rare situations where this may be the correct action—but it usually isn't.

God designed life and human relationships in such a way that each of us must learn to navigate social and relational struggles. Running from them is the wrong way to respond.

For most normal social conflict and relational stress, self-segregation and a defensive spirit is the wrong answer because it doesn't solve the problem or resolve the conflict, it merely abandons from it. Working through stuff requires humility, sincerity, and biblical wisdom—and it leads to growth, reconciliation, and selfless, Christlike love.

God Highly Values People and Relationships

Nothing on earth is more important than relationships—and God's Word makes it clear that above all He wants us to have right relationships. Jesus repeatedly commanded us to *love one another.* He must have known this would be a continual challenge.

"A new commandment I give unto you, That ye love one another; as I have loved you, that ye also love one another" (John 13:34).

"This is my commandment, That ye love one another, as I have loved you" (John 15:12).

"These things I command you, that ye love one another" (John 15:17).

Much of the New Testament instruction to the local church involves the interpersonal relationships of Christians. We are commanded to work through things, to forgive, to be tenderhearted, to forebear one another in love, to serve one another in love, to submit to one another, and to be gentle, long suffering, and gracious. We are commanded to do everything within our power to live peaceably with all men and to pursue peace with all men.

These responses are such a different portrait than the carnal and vicious responses that Christians often pour out upon one another over the most trivial of matters. We are so often un-Christlike. And never are we tempted to be more so than when we feel that our children have been handled unjustly by a peer or an authority figure. Few things reveal our flesh more quickly and vociferously than when we defend our offended child.

Yet, one of the most critical ways we help our children grow is by allowing them to work through these struggles rather than swooping in to segregate and sanitize them. And *our* relationships are *their* models. They learn from our examples—by watching our reactions and responses.

How are you helping your young person handle relational conflict and navigate social difficulty?

Three Types of Teens

I'm not a psychologist, but I do minister to young people and their families—a lot. Generally, I see three types of teens relationally or socially:

Relationally/socially dominant—these are kids who are outgoing but unrestrained. They jump into the center of attention and stay there—even if it requires them to be rude and thoughtless. They are loud, undiscerning, and controlling. If the social world isn't revolving around them, they work to make it so. Their social growth needs temperance. They need to learn that the world doesn't revolve around them.

Relationally/socially passive—these are kids who withdraw from social interaction and wait for the world to be friendly to them. Their unfriendliness flows from insecurity. They are self-focused and good at blaming everybody else for being unfriendly. They are easy to not notice because they *try* to be invisible, and then often play the victim when they are overlooked. Socially immature, they need to be coached and instructed in principles of biblical friendship and selflessness.

Relationally/socially balanced—these are the kids whose social and relational skills are developing with reasonable maturity (for their age). All teens have insecurities, but theirs do not typically paralyze them. They participate in conversations and group fellowship without having to control them or be the center of them. They have friends because they show themselves friendly (Proverbs 18:24). In these teens, there is a functional balance (usually rooted in Christ and family) that allows them to seek out, develop, and maintain reasonable and healthy friendships and interpersonal relationships.

Please note—every teen has some immaturity that results in social conflict and relational breakdown. But all three types above (and their parents) tend to handle or respond to that conflict differently.

The *relationally/socially dominant* tend to create or attract social struggle with others who are also dominant, which can lead to personal offense and intense conflict without a mind for resolution. The goal here is *winning, not resolving.* These individuals and families tend toward escalating the conflict until many others are involved, hurts are increasing, and some final relational explosion occurs (e.g., "Fine, we're leaving this school/youth group/church!").

The *relationally/socially passive* tend to find themselves alone and segregated (by their own spirit of withdrawal) but then complain and blame everybody else. Rather than grow in godly love and in serving others, these families tend to withdraw further. "Since my child doesn't have any friends in this environment, I will segregate him or her, because it must be the environment's fault." Again, in rare occasions the environment can certainly contribute, but this blaming the environment is usually the wrong first step. Examining my own child's social maturity and behavior is the wise first step, but the passive group leans toward self-segregation as the first and only answer.

The *relationally/socially balanced* tend to work through interpersonal conflict, or their parents require them to. For instance, these parents don't allow blame-shifting. They put the burden of social growth and conflict resolution on their own child's shoulders and expect them to take personal responsibility for dealing with and responding rightly to social struggles. These parents may say something like, "I'm sorry you're having a tough time at school. Let's work together to understand it, work through it, and see how we can learn to love others like Jesus does." As a result, this group tends to grow through and work through troubles rather than run from them.

Consider those three very different approaches before you read on. Which one are you and your children? Are you helping your child to become relationally and socially balanced?

Principles for Growing through Social Strife

There are a million different scenarios, and every circumstance has different dynamics. For this reason, it's impossible to exhaustively address this subject in a short chapter. Let's explore some guiding principles that will help you lead your teen from social strife to spiritual maturity.

Social strife and conflict are inevitable where there are people. No human environment is free from social strife. Helping our children respond rightly to social problems will help them relate well with all sorts of people for the rest of their lives. Sheltering them from every social discomfort will merely keep them weak and vulnerable.

Our kids will work hard to fix blame upon others. None of my children have ever come home from school saying, "Dad, I'm unfriendly and relationally immature, and I'm burdened about my carnality and how I mistreat people." They always want to say it's someone else's fault. And we are all very good at telling a story in our own favor. See through this. Be willing to be a shoulder to cry on, but don't constantly help your child avoid taking responsibility or accepting blame.

Jesus' instruction for relational conflict is positive engagement. Look at His instructions in Luke 6:27–36:

"But I say unto you which hear, Love your enemies, do good to them which hate you, Bless them that curse you, and pray for them which despitefully use you. And unto him that smiteth thee on the one cheek offer also the other; and him that taketh away thy cloak forbid not to take thy coat also. Give to every man that asketh of thee; and of him that taketh away thy goods ask them not again. And as ye would that men should do to you, do ye also to them likewise. For if ye love them which love you, what thank have ye? for sinners also love those that love them. And if ye do good to them which do good to you, what thank have ye? for sinners also do even the same. And if ye lend to them of whom ye hope to receive, what thank have ye? for sinners also lend to sinners, to receive as much again. But love ye your enemies, and do good, and lend, hoping for nothing again; and your reward shall be great, and ye shall be the children of the Highest: for he is kind unto the unthankful and to the evil. Be ye therefore merciful, as your Father also is merciful."

When we are willfully mistreated, Jesus instructs us to turn it around through positive engagement…

- Love them that hurt you.
- Do good to them that hate you.
- Bless them that spite you.
- Give to them that take from you.
- Do good to them as God the Father has done to you.
- Be merciful as God has shown you mercy.

Do you lead your child to respond biblically or carnally? Does your response tend toward grace or "get-even"? Do your reactions lead your child to react in the flesh or in the Spirit?

Social strife requires a practical approach. Here are some practical steps that may help you respond well and lead your child to do the same.

Pray for wisdom and discernment. There is always more to the story than you can see. You need to see God's perspective and help your child grow in Christlikeness.

Have realistic (not idealistic) expectations of people environments. If you expect your church, youth group, or school to be free of such struggles, that's not realistic. You are setting yourself up for disappointment.

Expect that your family member shares as much blame as the others. In the vast majority of teen conflicts, both parties have sinned and mistreated the other. "Who started it" is generally irrelevant by the time the conflict shows up on your radar.

Don't react to perceptions or misunderstandings. Too often we speak first and think later. We react before we know the whole story. Cast down imaginations (2 Corinthians 10:5), don't overreact, but seek to know the truth and understand the big picture.

Look in the mirror first and take heed unto thyself. Generally speaking, if *you* offend me, the problem is *me*. Psalm 119:165 teaches, *"Great peace have they which love thy law: and nothing shall offend them."* It would be hard for you to offend me if I'm not easily offended.

See every conflict as an opportunity to learn to love like Jesus. These moments are great teaching moments (e.g., "Jesus is giving you a chance to learn how to love someone who wasn't nice to you…").

Lead your family to respond biblically, not spitefully. Plan a response that honors the Lord and edifies others. Bake the offender some brownies—everybody knows it's impossible to be angry with someone who bakes you brownies.

Be patient through the hard seasons. Even when my child is at fault, these conflicts are difficult. Be a good listener and have an understanding heart. You can comfort the distressed without condoning sinful or self-centered responses.

Be approachable as a parent and a team player with other parents. Have a humble, team spirit with other parents and work together toward resolution. Don't accuse.

Refuse to let emotions make the decisions. Your emotions or your child's emotions should not be in the driver's seat of these situations. If your child's emotions have the power to stir you up against other Christian brothers, you have given those emotions too much power.

Refuse to take up your child's offense. My wrong reaction justifies the child's wrong reaction. Wise parents settle emotions rather than stirring them up. Your child's emotional response will be in direct proportion to yours.

Continue to respond biblically with patient endurance. Growth in these areas is sometimes slow and lasts for a season. Keep hitting the reset button and hang in there until you get through it—and you will!

Enlist the help of godly mediators. When helpful, have a youth pastor or teacher help mediate a resolution between offended parties. Neutral voices can sometimes mediate a less emotional solution.

When My Kid Is Wrong

I have had many difficult appointments with parents and authorities over the years. Sometimes I've *been* the embarrassed parent whose children have misbehaved. Other times I've tried to comfort or encourage another embarrassed parent whose children have misbehaved. These are not fun moments, but they are crucial to the growth and development of our children.

This comes back to *partnering* with authorities whom you can trust to influence your family biblically. Authority must be united in a child's life, and the enemy will work hard to break down that unity. There will be misunderstandings, emotions, and embarrassment that should be worked through.

Three Principles Relating to Other Authorities

Let your child's authorities hold them accountable. It is of utmost importance that you not allow your teen to divide you against his other authorities—teachers, coaches, principal, etc. Be supportive and stand together with those authorities. If for some reason you can't trust them, then you have placed your child under the wrong authorities. Find some you can trust.

Let your child bear the full responsibility and consequences for their behavior. When our kids get into trouble, we need to let them "face the music." This produces growth and character even though it's unpleasant and maybe embarrassing. When our kids have hurt their testimony, we need to let them work to restore it and deal with the negative consequences of their actions. In the end it's worth it.

Let your child know you are there for them to help and encourage. It's important for your kids to know you are always working toward their best interests and supporting them—even though you stand with their authorities. You can let them "face the music" without rejecting them personally or further discouraging them. Give them hope and help through the tough times.

A bad name often brings with it false accusations, which are hard for a kid to grasp. If your teen has hurt his name, it will take time to recover. Work to give them hope even while they endure the painful consequences. In time they can restore their good name and regain the trust they have lost. Often kids expect instant *trust* to accompany instant *forgiveness*. *Forgiveness* can be instant. *Trust* takes time to rebuild. One can be *forgiven* without being *trusted*. Help them understand the difference.

When Authority Is Wrong

In the rare occasions when you genuinely feel that an authority is missing something or is simply wrong, don't let your child know that at first. Go privately to the authority, with a humble spirit, ask their input, and see their side of the story. Then try to share your perspective and cooperate together for the good of your child. If your spirit is right and the authority's spirit is right, you should be able to work together to help your teen take responsibility and lead him or her to growth and maturity. If the authority is genuinely wrong, they should be willing to speak with your teen personally to make things right through an apology.

In the very rare occasion when an authority figure has clearly and openly violated biblical principles, don't cover it up and don't pretend to support it. Respect the position of authority but clearly reject sinful or unwise behavior. Teach your child to love and honor the person but also to understand where that person sinned or acted unwisely. Supporting unbiblical behavior in an authority figure is confusing to our kids—and it ultimately makes them resentful. Honor God above all—that's the ultimate standard.

In the sad instances where you have discovered that authority has been abusive and broken the law—call the police immediately and cooperate fully with legal authorities and biblical counselors. I pray this never happens to your family.

Interventions and conflicts with authorities can be emotional. Don't be led by your emotions, and don't be led by your child's emotions. Be led by principle, respect, and responsibility. Be willing to let your child be disciplined biblically, and don't defend or rationalize bad behavior—even if you are embarrassed by it.

Preparing the Path or the Child?

Over two decades of student ministry, we have witnessed a lot of social and relational conflict. And there are a couple of overarching observations:

Socially—Teenagers who mistreated each other, when parents lead them to grow rather than run, often grow up to be very good friends. Working through it is always the best most Christ-honoring response.

Behaviorally—Parents who face bad behavior head on with a humble, cooperative spirit toward their child's authorities always help their children.

Don't run from conflict. Don't run from trouble. Grow through it. Let your child grow through it. Yes, they will struggle. Yes, they will hurt. Don't dismiss the hurt uncaringly, but don't overreact either.

Don't be a defensive parent. You will dramatically stunt your child's spiritual growth.

Choose to be a peaceable parent—and to guide your child in learning the skills of being a peacemaker and being peaceable.

You've probably heard the story of the boy who decided to help a struggling butterfly out of its cocoon by cutting it open. In doing so, he removed the struggle that would have prepared the butterfly for flight. Even so, there are some struggles that our children need as they prepare for adulthood—and wise parents will allow the struggle to prepare the child.

It has been said, "Many parents are working hard to prepare the path for their children. Wise parents are working hard to prepare their children for the path."

You cannot control the path, but you can prepare your child.

19

THE CORRECTIVE PARENT
Winning My Child's Heart through Chastening

Discipline is a holy thing. Too often we parents take discipline lightly or treat it flippantly. In the big picture, all discipline is about bringing our children into a right relationship with their Heavenly Father that He might bless their lives. It's not about controlling behavior, modifying behavior, or minimizing embarrassment.

Pure and simple, it's about bringing them into proper alignment with the heart, ways, and favor of their gracious Heavenly Father.

"Honour thy father and thy mother, as the LORD thy God hath commanded thee; that thy days may be prolonged, and that it may go well with thee, in the land which the LORD thy God giveth thee" (Deuteronomy 5:16).

Discipline is sacred. Correcting another life is a grave responsibility. In some ways, I wish this wasn't a part of parenting or spiritual leadership. Yet, it is, by God's design. He has ordained that a large part of your job description involves *correction*.

The premise of this chapter is simple. Biblically correcting your child is one of the greatest ways to win their hearts to you and to God, forever.

You see, intuitively and subconsciously, your child knows that it is your responsibility to correct their course and direct them into righteousness. When you do, they know you love them. When you don't, they intuitively feel unloved and neglected. It's a bit of a paradox, but it's true. The very thing that causes their greatest temporary displeasure and unhappiness—your correction—is also one of the things that makes them feel most loved and secure. Biblical correction is one of their greatest needs and deep desires.

"Get off my case and leave me alone!"—that's their spoken cry.

"Love me enough to save me from myself!"—that's their unspoken cry.

"Chasten thy son while there is hope, and let not thy soul spare for his crying" (Proverbs 19:18).

Before We Discipline Our Children

With these thoughts in mind, there are two critical questions I must ask myself before entering into any discipline with my children.

1. Am I right with my Heavenly Father? It would be rather hypocritical to try to bring my child into a relationship that I will not bring myself into. It would be completely duplicitous to demand submission from my children if I myself am not submissive.

I cannot expect my child to love, obey, and honor a God that I will not.

I challenge you to begin all family discipline with this question. Search *your* heart before you correct *theirs*. This will help you stay right with the Lord. It will make your discipline *authentic*. It will give you a spirit of humility in meeting out discipline. It will give you a right perspective of your role as you are "under the authority" of your own Heavenly Father.

2. Am I right with my child? This one is as critical as the first. For discipline to be received, it must transfer far more than mere punishment or rebuke. It must transfer love and compassion. It must transfer care. It must transfer the heart of Christ and a passionate desire for "what is broken to be made whole." It must be redemptive in nature. This cannot happen if there is an unresolved offense between my child and me.

For many parents, the way they deal out discipline actually *creates* deeper offense. We yell, scream, throw fits, and generally spout unrestrained anger. All of this is *counter productive* to biblical discipline. While it may temporarily curb undesired behavior (at least in our presence) it actually makes matters much worse under the surface—in the heart.

Authentic discipline only takes place when my heart is completely right with my child. Trying to throw down discipline on top of previous offense only builds and feeds a spirit of resentment. This merely invites my child to despise me.

If my own sin is standing in the way, I cannot deal authentically with my child's—and the child intuitively knows this.

The Sweetness of Discipline

Discipline is not only sacred—it is *precious*. It doesn't need to be purely unpleasant. It can actually be sweet, restorative, rebuilding, and renewing. It can bring wholeness to that which was broken, sweetness to that which was bitter, and closeness to that which was distant.

Biblical discipline brings a life "out of fellowship" back into fellowship. It puts joyful delight and warmth back into a cold relationship.

In short—biblical discipline *heals*. This is exactly what Hebrews 12 teaches regarding chastening.

If you desire your discipline to be these things, you must first provide a "YES" to these two simple questions—*Am I right with my Heavenly Father? Am I right with my child?* Rest assured, if these two things are in place, your discipline will find its way into the heart and have a life-transforming effect.

Here's a quick litmus test—hug your child and pray with them after you correct. If your teen responds with warmth, that's a good sign that you provided biblical discipline with the heart of Christ. If not, sit down and talk it out. Don't stop pursuing an open heart and relational warmth, even after a moment of unpleasant discipline. Discipline done right should bring your relationship closer almost immediately.

Ten Principles for Winning Your Child's Heart with Discipline

How can we discipline our children in a way that wins their hearts? Here are ten principles for handling discipline biblically:

Discipline that develops the heart...

1. Is controlled and premeditated—It doesn't fly off the handle or out of control.

"He that is slow to anger is better than the mighty; and he that ruleth his spirit than he that taketh a city" (Proverbs 16:32).

"Fathers, provoke not your children to anger, lest they be discouraged" (Colossians 3:21).

2. Is biblically principled and corrective—It rests upon a Higher Authority—God and His Word. It is compassionately firm and isn't easily manipulated. It connects biblical principles and instruction to the whole circumstance.

"Chasten thy son while there is hope, and let not thy soul spare for his crying" (Proverbs 19:18).

"All scripture is given by inspiration of God, and is profitable for doctrine, for reproof, for correction, for instruction in righteousness" (2 Timothy 3:16).

3. Is instructive and nurturing—It moves beyond reaction and actually instructs and trains.

"Hear, ye children, the instruction of a father, and attend to know understanding. For I give you good doctrine, forsake ye not my law. For I was my father's son, tender and only beloved in the sight of my mother. He taught me also, and said unto me, Let thine heart retain my words: keep my commandments, and live" (Proverbs 4:1–4).

4. Is focused on beliefs then behavior—It seeks to understand the beliefs that drive behavior, not merely change behavior. It addresses the root, not merely the fruit.

"My son, give me thine heart, and let thine eyes observe my ways" (Proverbs 23:26).

"Hear, ye children, the instruction of a father, and attend to know understanding. For I give you good doctrine, forsake ye not my law" (Proverbs 4:1–2).

5. Is focused on restoring relationships—It always seeks a stronger relationship, not a wounded one. When a relationship is wounded, it doesn't rest until it is reconciled.

"Fathers, provoke not your children to anger, lest they be discouraged" (Colossians 3:21).

6. Is listening and encouraging—It contemplates, considers, and listens to the feelings and expressions of the heart. It seeks to know the whole story and to be fair and just. Unjust discipline leads to resentment and bitterness.

"Like as a father pitieth his children, so the Lord pitieth them that fear him" (Psalm 103:13).

"Fathers, provoke not your children to anger, lest they be discouraged" (Colossians 3:21).

"As you know how we exhorted and comforted and charged every one of you, as a father doth his children" (1 Thessalonians 2:11).

7. Is prayerful and Christ-centered—It brings Christ to the forefront and maintains a humble spirit.

"Confess your faults one to another, and pray one for another, that ye may be healed. The effectual fervent prayer of a righteous man availeth much" (James 5:16).

8. Is selfless and contextual—It is for the profit of the child and helps the child see the larger context of blessing. It doesn't make mountains out of molehills and doesn't leave the child feeling like a total failure.

"For they verily for a few days chastened us after their own pleasure; but he for our profit, that we might be partakers of his holiness" (Hebrews 12:10).

9. Is forward looking—It blesses the heart with hope and an "I believe in you" spirit. It ends with hopefulness—"You are a great kid and I know God is growing you through this!"

"Hear, O my son, and receive my sayings; and the years of thy life shall be many" (Proverbs 4:10).

"As newborn babes, desire the sincere milk of the word, that ye may grow thereby" (1 Peter 2:2).

10. Is obedient to a Higher Authority—It flows from a heart that is obviously obedient to the Heavenly Father.

"My son, fear thou the LORD and the king: and meddle not with them that are given to change" (Proverbs 24:21).

"My son, give me thine heart, and let thine eyes observe my ways" (Proverbs 23:26).

Understanding Biblical Chastening

"Now no chastening for the present seemeth to be joyous, but grievous: nevertheless afterward it yieldeth the peaceable fruit of righteousness unto them which are exercised thereby" (Hebrews 12:11).

Christian parents often confuse the concepts of *punishment* and *chastening*. Biblically, these things are very different.

Punishment is punitive. *Chastening* is restorative.

Punishment is punitive. It is always about paying for a crime. It condemns and separates as a result of a crime or offense.

What did we do as a child when we knew we were going to be punished? We ran. We hid. We lied. We blame-shifted. We rationalized. We did everything we could to avoid being "caught" and punished. This is the natural human response when punishment is looming—do anything to avoid being punished. But biblical chastening is very different.

Chastening is restorative. It is always about growth and forward development. It doesn't condemn; it corrects. It doesn't condone sin; it calls the sinner away from sin and into blessing.

Remember Jesus with the woman caught in adultery? *"Neither do I condemn thee, go and sin no more"* (John 8:11). The word *chastening* in Hebrews 12 is the same word as *nurture* in Ephesians 6—it refers to the whole training and development of the child. It is growth oriented. It is about yielding *"the peacable fruit of righteousness"* (Hebrews 12:11).

Parent, we need to know the difference between these two words, and we need to teach them to our children. If we view our discipline as purely punitive, we are completely missing grace and redemption! God doesn't punish you or me when we sin—He punished Jesus *for us*. But He does *chasten* us—He is interested in calling us away from sin and its power, and helping us grow—be transformed into the image of Jesus Christ. He is interested in our greater blessing!

If we view our discipline as merely punitive, we will rationalize our outbursts of anger rather than repent of them. We will view the whole encounter with a harder disposition than we should. We will rule with an iron, authoritarian fist and completely miss the tender growth and development that God desires to bring about through our Spirit-filled correction.

God's anger was already poured out at the cross. But His chastening is an ongoing process in our lives.

If we understand chastening, we know it is uncomfortable. We know it is a miserable experience for both parent and child—but it is motivated by godly grace, unconditional love, and the ultimate best interest of the child. If we understand the concept of chastening, we will pursue restoration, reconciliation, and redemption between our child and God and our child and us.

If our children understand chastening versus punishment, they will know our heart of love in the midst of unpleasant confrontation. They will know we are not merely pouring out our "hot displeasure" (Hebrews 12:10), but we are nurturing their lives for the Lord—even if the experience, the discussion, or the confrontation is painful or uncomfortable.

Be sure that you and your child understand the difference between *chastening* and *punishment*.

Chastening says, "I truly love you and want what's best for you."

Punishment simply says, "I'm angry at you, and now you have to pay!"

The two are very, very different.

Contextualizing the Correction

One final admonition before we close this chapter. Teenagers don't know how to contextualize your correction. Here's what I mean.

With all of our children, correction is always unpleasant. In my sons' or daughter's minds, when Mom or Dad is displeased, all of life is on general meltdown. The overriding message in their heart is, "I'm a failure!"

Often, we are dealing with an isolated aspect of character or behavior in a child who is doing very well in many other areas of life before God. In our minds as parents, we see and know this. We would give them an A+ in so many areas of life. "But today, we're dealing with the class you are failing."

They don't make this differentiation. In their minds, "If my parents are unhappy in one area, then I'm failing in all of life!" And also in their minds they think, "You probably never had these struggles or failed these classes when you were a kid!" Do you see the problem that could develop here? Utter despair. Discouragement. "I can't win. I'm a total loser."

It is vital in your discipline that you define the context and that you share your own struggles as a kid. If something is big, let them know it's big. If it's little, let them know it's little. Help them know how you grew through this same struggle. They need to know that they are not alone and that they are not utter failures. *They need hope.*

Help them see that a failure in one area isn't a general failure in all areas. Don't let the enemy get a foothold of discouragement in their hearts. Remind them, in spite of a failure, that there are many successes.

Parent, we all fail at times in the area of discipline. One flawed, sinful being correcting another is a recipe for mistakes. We all lose our patience when we feel that we are correcting the same irresponsible behavior over and over again. When you fail to discipline biblically, simply repent and make it right with God and your child. Then proceed to be the right kind of authority in a spirit of biblical chastening.

By God's grace, we can all grow into more Christlike, gracious parents who mete out correction with *tough love* and *tender hearts*.

20

THE HURTING PARENT
Keep Fattening the Calf

What can you do when your growing or grown children begin to stray spiritually? We've seen a lot of parents hurt, mystified, and shaken by sudden and radical spiritual changes in the lives of their young adult children. One day, I may be one of them. It would be arrogant and presumptuous to think otherwise.

Having a wayward child hurts—beyond hurt. To a parent, this is an ache and wound of a depth that words cannot describe. And yet, where there is God and grace, there is always hope. Perhaps this chapter should have come earlier in the book. Perhaps it's a fitting way to conclude. But let's consider God's ointment to salve the wounds when parenting hurts.

The Wrong Responses

When things go bad, desperate parents start to react rather than respond. Emotion takes over and *bad* becomes *worse*.

Control—In these painful moments, some parents grasp for control—trying to maintain a mythical stranglehold of childhood authority. This always escalates a situation to become worse and creates greater distance relationally and spiritually. Overreacting in emotional and reactionary dominance doesn't work.

Resignation—In a wild swing to the other extreme, some parents abandon their post of parental influence and retreat into discouragement, feeling like failures. They mentally, emotionally, and spiritually disconnect with an "oh well" resignation, as if there is nothing they can really do.

Discouragement—Some just turn inward and mourn their loss. Discouragement becomes overwhelming. The enemy seizes the opportunity to highlight every personal flaw and screams blame into our hearts and minds as the venomous accuser that he is.

Anger—Still others respond in anger—returning hurt for hurt. Angry emails, angry voice mails, angry text messages, angry gossip—it becomes a nasty and bloody fire-fight where words and actions inflict wounds that last for decades.

None of these responses are helpful or truthful—not one.

The Right Responses

Recently, Dana and I were privileged to prayerfully and fearfully sit down with two sets of parents who were facing circumstances in which we all felt powerless. It was an overwhelming set of circumstances. We wept together. We prayed together. We looked desperation and discouragement directly in the eye as it taunted us and waved its victory flag in our faces. For a long time we waited on God, feeling utterly hopeless and fighting despair.

After several days, a lot of prayer, a long drive, a three-hour dinner, and the powerful intervention of the grace of God—together, we rediscovered the weapons God has given us to fight battles that are far beyond our human control. And together, we saw God work a miracle.

There are times when parenting young adults becomes incredibly and indescribably painful. The enemy screams in your face, "I have won!" You seem to have lost all influence. You feel as though you are a complete and utter failure as a parent. The immediate loss seems permanent and unrecoverable. It's as though a lifetime of parental love, labor, and sacrifice is lost in a moment.

Please read these words carefully: the battle is not over. You are not a failure unless you choose to be. There is *always, always hope in God's grace.* The story is still being written!

Temporary loss does not equal permanent failure. If you've become the parent of a prodigal, you have entered into a very critical time. What you do next, and throughout this season, is of paramount importance. The rest of the story has yet to be told—and it will take decades to write. Are you up for a level of spiritual parenting like you've never imagined?

Here are the first three things you need to do:

Relinquish control. You do not have control, and you won't. You can't. An adult is an adult. Our kids grow up, and God has given them free wills. The best of parents still raise children with free wills, and sometimes those children make bad choices. Some really bad parents raise children who make good choices. Free will is real. We do not have control, and we have no absolute guarantee that our kids will choose to do right. And once they are adults, our authority is massively diminished in their lives.

A part of a prodigal's agenda is to assert *control*—to thrust in the face of authority that they no longer have power. Accept it. Acknowledge it. "You are an adult and accountable before God." That's the truth. When you relinquish control, you catch your adult offspring off guard. They weren't expecting you to surrender your authority without a fight. They were bunkered down and ready for your assault.

When you relinquish control, you remove yourself from the power-struggle, and your young adult stands squarely accountable to God alone. This is a much higher, much more grave, much more powerful accountability. This would set any human being on their heels. You have defanged and defused one of their primary justifications for rebellion.

Repent of known sin or perceived wounding. If there is a wound or resentment between you and your child that is in any way driving or justifying this behavior in their mind—repent of it before the Lord and your child. Just deal with it, regardless of the response or the reason. Remove the impetus of the bad behavior, regardless of whether or not it is legitimate.

Usually a part of the agenda of rebellion in a prodigal is to return hurt—to wound the one who has wounded me. Often there are years of wounding that perhaps a parent didn't even know about. Sometimes it's clear abuse or neglect. Other times it is purely perception in the mind of the child. Either way, perception is reality. If I perceive that you have hurt me, you may as well have. And to win me, we're going to have to reconcile that hurt and begin the healing process.

When you reach out and acknowledge hurt (even if you didn't intentionally create it or know about it) and ask forgiveness, you have taken away another major leg of rationale for self-destructive behavior.

Respond with grace—Prodigals are expecting backlash. They are expecting rejection. They have played this all out in their mind. They know how it will go. They have built a case, argued it, and convicted you guilty on all counts—before the story even began. When you respond with carnality in kind, the case is closed by your harsh or defensive response.

When you respond with grace in *kindness,* the case is disrupted. Previous evidence—imagination—becomes inadmissible. When you (the parent) refuse to be angry, to argue, to overreact, or to freak-out, you are paving the way for conviction and reconciliation. A gracious response allows God to be God, and allows Him to deal with His child His way— by His Spirit and His Word.

Putting God's child in God's hands to deal with His way frees you to be a minister of grace to your own son or daughter even though they have hurt you deeply. I promise you—this, they are not expecting.

This is the most Christlike form of parental love that is ever expressed. As we nailed Him to the cross, Jesus cried, "Father, forgive them…." That was His response to you and to me—to our rejection and despising of Him. A cross-like grace will catch your prodigal completely off guard. Calvary's love will work in ways that nothing else could. After all, consider how you came to Christ. Grace worked in your life, didn't it?

Grace is truly *amazing!*

Weapons of Amazing Grace

These are the grace weapons that God gives us all to use against impossible circumstances:

Unconditional love and acceptance—Regardless of what my child does, how my child hurts me, or how far out of bounds my child behaves—I will choose to respond with Christlike compassion and unconditional love. This is a powerful weapon that speaks to the heart and the conscience. This is a Calvary kind of love. This is the Gospel lived out in human relationships.

By the way, acceptance of a person does not equal approval of sin.

Godly grace—Regardless of what my child has done, I extend grace—unmerited favor. Just as grace is God's response to my sin, grace will be my response to my child's sin. Grace is always undeserved, and it is the most powerful resource for creating an environment where repentance and change are possible.

Intercessory prayer—This weapon brings all the powers of Heaven to work in the situation. It is the single most powerful and yet most neglected response to any strained relationship. As I pray, God will work. He will respond to my faith and intervene at a depth I could never see.

God's Word—Opinions and personal preferences matter little, but the principles of God's Word are powerful. When battles of the will only escalate a situation, the principles of God's Word speak to the heart with the potential of lasting life change. If your son or daughter will speak with you, speak truth in loving terms. Share principles with compassion.

Patient endurance—Change takes time. Repentance is rarely instantaneous. Parents who win these battles *never* give up (emphasis on *never*). They faithfully and persistently use these weapons until the battle is won. It may take ten months or ten years—they are never giving up.

These are weapons of the Spirit. These are the tools that God places into the hands of "Navy Seal" parents—parents of the highest order and caliber. These are rescuing parents. These are "secret ops" parents who engage in the most intense forms of battle. And these weapons are powerfully effective.

Weapons of the Flesh or of the Spirit

Weapons of the flesh will react. Weapons of the Spirit will respond.

Weapons of flesh will lash out. Weapons of the Spirit will reach out.

Weapons of flesh desire retribution. Weapons of the Spirit desire reconciliation.

Weapons of flesh will seek control. Weapons of the Spirit will seek influence.

Weapons of flesh will make demands. Weapons of the Spirit will make pleas.

Weapons of flesh will accuse. Weapons of the Spirit will accept.

Weapons of flesh will return hurt. Weapons of the Spirit will return grace.

Weapons of flesh will argue. Weapons of the Spirit will reason.

Here they are again:

- Unconditional love
- Godly grace
- Intercessory prayer
- God's Word
- Patient endurance

We see them in the life of the prodigal's father in Luke 15. Read the story:

"And he said, A certain man had two sons: And the younger of them said to his father, Father, give me the portion of goods that falleth to me. And he divided unto them his living. And not many days after the younger son gathered all together, and took his journey into a far country, and there wasted his substance with riotous living. And when he had spent all, there arose a mighty famine in that land; and he began to be in want. And he went and joined himself to a citizen of that country; and he sent him into his fields to feed swine. And he would fain have filled his belly with the husks that the swine did eat: and no man gave unto him. And when he came to himself, he said, How many hired servants of my father's have bread enough and to spare, and I perish with hunger! I will arise and go to my father,

and will say unto him, Father, I have sinned against heaven, and before thee, And am no more worthy to be called thy son: make me as one of thy hired servants. And he arose, and came to his father. But when he was yet a great way off, his father saw him, and had compassion, and ran, and fell on his neck, and kissed him. And the son said unto him, Father, I have sinned against heaven, and in thy sight, and am no more worthy to be called thy son. But the father said to his servants, Bring forth the best robe, and put it on him; and put a ring on his hand, and shoes on his feet: And bring hither the fatted calf, and kill it; and let us eat, and be merry: For this my son was dead, and is alive again; he was lost, and is found. And they began to be merry" (Luke 15:11–24).

Take hope, parent! If you are facing impossible circumstances and you feel hopeless and powerless, there is much you can do to fight a spiritual battle for your wayward child. God's work is not finished in your child's heart, and God's Word is still powerful to change lives. If you are fighting for a prodigal, adult child, you are also fighting for your grandchildren.

So take the long view, don't be discouraged, and stay in the fight.

Many, many prodigals return to the Lord over time. Don't lose hope.

Just keep fattening the calf—and keep looking out the front window with open arms.

CONCLUSION
Lord Jesus, Help Me Parent Like You!

I can't believe how quickly decades pass. A couple of years ago I was sitting on a red-eye flight with Dana, Larry, and Haylee—starting our twentieth family vacation—our first without Lance. My mind went back to what seemed like a moment ago.

"I've been here before," I thought. It was in a hotel room in Palm Desert, California about thirteen years ago—our last night of family vacation in another era. We had spent the day swimming, roller blading, mini-golfing—all the good stuff of a family vacation. The lazy day wound to a giggly close with two little boys—very little—jumping on the bed in their PJs, being tickled, and praying together.

As Mom whisked them off to brush their teeth, I faced a sudden rush of emotion, seemingly out of nowhere. It was an unexpected flash forward to a far off moment—a time when the two boys would be grown men and family vacations were, in themselves, winding to a close. As I imagined that "far away time" I fought off the emotion, but Dana caught my eye. She must have sensed something in my face. She turned, and with her winsome smile said, "Hey, are you okay?" I had succeeded at holding back the tears, until she said that.

I did the "man thing" and laughed off a couple of tears. Then Dana came and sat next to me asking what was up. "Nothing. I just realized, if God gives us eighteen family vacations with our first-born, then six of them are gone already. That's just not much time, really." And then, while the two boys who were supposed to be brushing teeth were obliviously splashing water and giggling a few feet away, we just sat on the bed, embraced each other, and shed a few tears, both feeling silly for doing so.

But that night on the red-eye flight it was real. That night we all loaded into the car and held our annual family tradition of many years— we listened to *You've Got A Friend in Me*. Once again, Dana started crying when she realized that one voice wasn't singing along as he always had in the past. And once again, I was reminded of how quickly the years have passed, and I'm thankful for every family vacation.

As I close the book, I have two overwhelming thoughts to share with you.

First, we don't have much time. It all goes very quickly, and once they're grown, you're not going to wish you had spent more time at the office while you had them.

Second, my teenagers (and pre-teen daughter) have literally become my best friends. I see them not only as my children, but as my friends, co-laborers, confidants, and spiritual-growth partners.

They challenge me in many ways. There are very few things in life as enjoyable as spending time with them—especially when we all sort of crash in the living room or on our bed and talk as a family and then pray together. Those are awesome times.

We should respect our kids. We should see them as unique creations—children of a perfect Heavenly Father. They are entrusted to my care for a short season, and then I must give them back to Him. Loving and nurturing them is a stewardship—a sacred trust. Enjoying life with them is one of the greatest gifts God could give. How brief a time we truly have with them.

Helping Our Kids Fall in Love with Their Heavenly Father

I believe our single greatest responsibility as parents is to love God and help our children love Him. If they truly love Him, they will live for Him and enjoy His best blessings in life. After all, this is the request of the young lady who wrote that sad letter shared at the beginning of this book. "Go for the heart and teach us to love God!" That's the cry of this generation—it's as though they are saying, "Be passionate for us!"

Recently, while away on a different family vacation, the Lord gave me some special moments with my kids. On one particular day, it seemed that God gave me some moments with Haylee that reminded me of my Heavenly Father. All day long, I kept seeing her longing for me as echoes of my own longings for my Heavenly Father, and I was reminded over and over of my desire to be more like *Him!* I fail too often.

When the day ended, I made a list of the "longings." These are the things I see and hear my children desire or need from me. These are also the things I desire from my Father. *He fulfills them perfectly.* Me? Not so much, but what a *great* Role Model we have. I think being a good parent flows from the continual attempt to express God's "fatherly heart" in our relationships with our own children.

I close this book with this list:

Dad, make special plans for me. On this particular day, the kids were excited that we had planned to rent a boat and a Sea-Doo. We had an awesome day of adventure on a beautiful lake. All three of my children hugged me and thanked me for planning the day. How our kids delight in the fact that Dad would actually make good plans for them!

I'm thankful that my Heavenly Father has planned more than a day—He has mapped out my whole life—including eternity—and His plan is always good!

Dad, protect me when I feel vulnerable. Haylee wouldn't ride the Sea-Doo with me until I promised her that I wouldn't scare her. (She knows that her brothers and I sometimes enjoy taunting her.) I promised her she could trust me. Riding the Sea-Doo was a scary experience that made her feel vulnerable and at risk. Things changed when she understood I would protect her on the journey.

How much more does my Heavenly Father assure me of His strong arms, marvelous grace, and loving care—no matter what I may face in life!

Dad, help me when I am afraid. Swimming in a lake and riding a Sea-Doo were both scary adventures for Haylee. She prefers a nice clean swimming pool that doesn't contain living things. Yet, early in the day, I felt that it was my responsibility, not to force her, but to help her face and overcome her fears. Together, we met those fears head-on and she soon discovered that they were unfounded. She soon understood that her fears were preventing her from enjoying much of what I had planned.

How thankful I am for a Heavenly Father who understands my fears and helps me face them and overcome them, that I might fully enjoy His plans for my life.

Dad, be strong where I am weak. When we first started out on the Sea-Doo together, I tried to let Haylee have the controls. She refused.

After a few moments though, we negotiated. "You put your hands on the handle-bars, and you control the speed," I said.

"Ok…" she said, "but you steer for me, that's my weakness!"

That struck me—"Dad, you be strong where I am weak."

I immediately thought of all of my debilitating weaknesses and human frailty, and I am grateful for a Heavenly Father who tells me that His strength is made perfect in weakness!

Dad, watch me and cheer me on. Within twenty minutes of being on that Sea-Doo, Haylee experienced a total transformation. Soon enough, I was holding on for dear life and she took control of both speed and direction. Her fears subsided, she was suddenly screaming with joy over the wind and water, "Hey Dad, watch this!" For the rest of the day she was commanding my attention, asking me to delight in her accomplishment. And every time I attempted to respond with pleasure.

It reminded me again of my Heavenly Father who looks upon me with His favor and showers me with thoughts of goodness and delight, in spite of myself.

Dad, listen to me when I need to talk. The day on the lake came to a close, the sun set, and I found myself sitting with Haylee on the back patio—just the two of us. She was radiant with memories of the wonderful day God had given to us. As we sat there under the stars, the night was quiet, and Haylee began to talk. Like any woman, she talked, and talked, and talked. And God seemed to say to me, "Just sit here and enjoy the sound of her voice—she's growing up fast!"

Aren't you thankful for a Heavenly Father who always listens to your voice and understands your heart's cry, who is never too busy or occupied to sit quietly with you as you pour out your heart?

Dad, show me faithfulness and consistency. Part of the evening conversation revolved around the start of school—Haylee was going into

6th grade. She was looking forward to her new teacher and a new year of growing. In talking about the challenges ahead, she complimented her new teacher and the positive reports that her brothers had given. In this, she made a simple statement that jumped out at me: "I know I'm going to like this teacher because I know what to expect!" She was complimenting the consistent and steadfast personality of which she had been told.

It reminded me that our kids long to see us be consistent and faithful to the things that matter. They long to know "what to expect" and their world becomes unstable when we live or act inconsistently.

Aren't you thankful for a Heavenly Father who is always the same?! With your Heavenly Father, you always know "what to expect!"

Dad, tell me about yourself. The conversation also turned to my childhood. "Dad, tell me about your favorite teacher. Why was she your favorite?" All too often, one of Haylee's "stay up later" strategies is to ask me to tell her a story about when I was a kid. I recalled all of my teachers and shared with her a few who were my favorites and why, and I was reminded again that our kids want to know us, to connect with us, and to relate with us in close and special ways.

I was also reminded of a Heavenly Father who gave me His living Word and tells me His story that I might know Him and relate to Him personally and closely every day!

Dad, wait with me when I need to pause. Finally, Haylee talked herself out and the conversation stopped—but not the togetherness. For some time we just sat there together, enjoying the evening breeze, looking at the stars, and being with each other. She wasn't demanding anything of me, and I wasn't demanding anything of her. We were just content being together.

I'm thankful for a Heavenly Father who loves me enough just to be there in my silence and reminds me of His presence.

Do you ever feel completely unqualified to parent the children God has blessed you with? Welcome to the club.

Yet, as parents, we sure are blessed with an *amazing* Role Model. Maybe if we spend more time with Him, we can become, to some small degree, the kind of father (parent) that He is. Perhaps He will help us to be accurate reflections of Him to our children.

Thanks for reading this book. I pray it will make a difference in your family.

May God bless you as you invest your life into passionate parenting!

As you pursue God with your whole heart, and pursue your child with your whole heart…

Most likely the two will meet!

"Behold, I have taught you statutes and judgments, even as the LORD *my God commanded me…"* (Deuteronomy 4:5).

ABOUT THE AUTHOR

CARY SCHMIDT serves as the senior pastor of Emmanual Baptist Church in Newington, Connecticut. He and his wife Dana have three children and enjoy serving the Lord and spending time together as a family. Cary's books include *Discover Your Destiny*, *Life Quest*, and others.

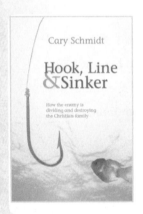
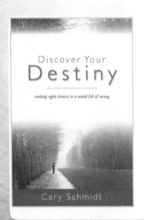

Visit us online

strivingtogether.com

wcbc.edu